MILITANT PARENTING

A
SURVIVAL GUIDE FOR PARENTS
WITH
PROBLEM KIDS

by

Dr. Jerry Brown

Jerry Brown

Internet Address:
DRJERRYBROWN@worldnet.att.net

Phone:714 639-4054
Fax: 714 639-3544

Library of Congress Cataloging

First Addition

ISBN # 0-9658304-0-3

ACKNOWLEDGMENT

No one understands what goes into writing a book better than a person who has done it. I have developed a new respect for authors who write prolifically, especially those who have been faithful to their craft over a period of many years. Theirs is truly a labor of love.

I wish to thank, Christina Peeve at Willow House Editing, f or her "militant" stand with me as I wrote the manuscript for this work. I will never forget her saying to me, "You can't write it that way; it is gross, and it will offend people," when I alluded to a silver spoon being misplaced in a person's body. Ironically, this book was written with the realization that many people may be offended during the process of parenting. That is its point. Someone is bound to be offended by what you do as a parent. This book shows you how to live with that inevitability.

I also wish to thank Dr. Al Truehart for his personal support and his computer expertise when I successively crashed my computers during this project, and Ron Webb for his graphic expertise and help with the pagination.

Most of all, I wish to thank my wife Lea, who continues to unconditionally love me and support my work in the field, even when it means sacrifices of time and resources to do so. Her greatest contribution has been her undying love and devotion to our amazing and wonderful children whom we love and have raised together.

DEDICATION

This book is dedicated to my four children (in order of appearance), Cammy, Michelle, Corey, and Mike, who have taught me much of what I know about parenting and much of what I needed to learn about life.

Jerry Brown
Orange, California

TABLE OF CONTENTS

CHAPTER ONE

THE MILITANT PARENT

A **MILITANT PARENT** is one who is willing to parent in ways of which some person or persons will not approve. In a sense, we are all Militant Parents when we endeavor to raise children, teenagers, and adults who still act like children or teenagers and not like adults.

The point here is that no matter what you do, some people will criticize you. Perhaps it will be your parents, perhaps your significant other's parents. Worse yet, it may be your partner. Sound familiar? Welcome to the crazy world of parenting!

Parenting is the most difficult job most of us will undertake in our lifetimes. We live in a society which offers certification and licensing for a variety of tasks and procedures. You must qualify for a license to drive a car following extensive training. You must earn a license to put on acrylic nails. But you don't have to have a license to parent.

Along with this non-licensed job come several twists which our culture imposes. Parenting is not only the most difficult job we will ever do; we can be prosecuted if we do it wrong! We may not be able to take any days off. If we do take days off, we may also be prosecuted, and we are held financially responsible for what our children and teenagers do. (More about that later.)

If this seems a bit negative, that's because it is! If successful parenting were easy, everyone would know how to do it. This is not to say its outcome is not rewarding. Parenting is potentially one of the most genuinely rewarding things in your life, but it can be mystifying, inconvenient and lonely, especially if you take to heart the criticism you are bound to receive in the course of trying to raise children in present-day society.

If you had no concerns about parenting, you would not be reading this book. If you are reading this book, you may already be in trouble parenting or trying to avoid further trouble. Here is an important reality related to the problem: WE as parents are the ones in trouble. What's wrong with this picture? Why isn't it they, or he or she? Well, I am glad you asked. One of the primary problems we deal with today as a culture is our tendency to allow the demonetization of parents.

DEMONIZATION OF PARENTS:

The current generation of parents has been confronted with a new view of parenting. Through authors like Alice Miller who wrote FOR THEIR OWN GOOD, we are getting a new view of the toxic side of parenting. Therapy, movies, articles, and public service agencies like Child Protective Services all contribute to a climate of concern about parenting and its many potential abuses. This contribution is a necessary one whose time has come. We now provide children and our culture with more protection from abusive parents, and it is no longer easy for an abusive parent to treat a child as chattel and owned property. This is a positive move toward protecting the human rights of people who have no legal means or resources to protect themselves.

With all this in mind, we must look at the possibility that the pendulum has swung too far in the other direction. Have we taught parents that to place <u>any</u> discipline or consequences on a child is an act of child abuse? The saddest thing therapists like myself see in consulting rooms and correctional systems are children who do not suffer consequences and are allowed to get away with acting out and other irresponsible behavior. It's a rough world for a teenager who has turned 18 (the adult age in California) and is confronted with an adult criminal justice system which is far more punitive and provides far less treatment than the juvenile correctional justice system.

This process of setting strict, perhaps even abusive limits and then retreating to a position of excessive leniency may be part of a cycle. Everything goes in cycles. To survive we must be "cycleologists" and examine our historical roots, as well as deal with old stereotypes when they reoccur.

Many issues involved in modern parenting are confusing. Corporal punishment is an example of a parental limit that is undergoing scrutiny and possible change. One of the best examples of this phenomenon today is the California legislature's attempt to place into law the right of a school administrator to paddle a child if he or she acts out. It is significant to note that it has taken the education system, parents, and mental health professionals twenty years to accept and formalize the idea that the only punishment <u>a parent</u> may safely use is AN OPEN HAND ON A CLOTHED BUTT. This guideline will keep Child Protective Services from knocking on your door. If you slap, beat, or otherwise leave bruises or marks on a child, you are subject to the wrath of the state. The "open hand" guideline represents progress in parental discipline.

But can you imagine the confusion if we now allow school administrators to <u>paddle</u> our children? You can see from pondering the corporal punishment issue why there is so much frustration among parents, professional child care workers, and law enforcement about what constitutes acceptable and unacceptable adult discipline of children.

Isn't physical punishment the same behavior for which Child Protective Services intervenes? Is there a quantifiable system from 1-10 that will specify how severely an administrator is to punish? Can someone measure the intensity of a swat as mild or heavy, soft or hard, stemming from rage or delivered with restraint? Not a chance.

I am personally pleased that California, like most other states, provides protection for children. State law goes further to define child workers (nurses, counselors, teachers, therapists, and doctors) as being <u>mandated by law</u> to report child abuse. If these professionals fail to do so, <u>they</u> can be prosecuted for failing to report. Further, if they do so, they are protected from prosecution. In all the thirty-one years I have worked as a therapist, probation officer, and parent educator, I have seen only positive outcomes from the multiple incidences with which I have worked in which child abuse has been reported. The imposition of child abuse laws has helped many parents to realize the limits they can and cannot use in physically dealing with their children.

If the experts can't make up their minds as to their stand on corporal punishment, pity the confused parents. I hope to tackle some of these issues in the chapters to come. You can already see what you are up against. To parent, you must battle through a complex set of theories, attitudes, laws, and opinions.

To parent successfully, you must <u>think</u> for yourself and be willing to be a MILITANT PARENT, and perhaps later, a Militant Grandparent.

So...What <u>do</u> you <u>do</u> about your critics? Ignore them? Explain that they should MTOB (mind their own business)? This is the dilemma we all face. The issue is, in many instances, to keep the *alternatives* coming in from those we love and respect, but to insist that they leave the driving to us. In the end, at some point in our children's lives, we must take a back seat and leave the driving to them. They will be on their own.

Here's an example: Martha Mom has a devoted mother. Martha herself was an obedient and conforming kid growing up and caused no problems for her parents. Her son Paul, however, inherited the energy level of both grandparents and his mother and father combined. The kid needs special limits, firmness, consistency, <u>and </u>medication. Grandmother does not agree with Martha Mom about Paul's medication, having read an alarming article on Ritalin in a parenting magazine. Consequently, Martha Mom must find a way, tactfully, to tell her mother that she loves her, appreciates her feedback, but has to manage Paul's childhood differently from how grandmother would have handled Paul had he been born in the 1960s.

It is not inconsistent to say to someone, " I love you Mom, and I know you love me and my children, but we have to do this our way, and it's not going to always be your way."

Even physicians and child psychologist or counselors may offer you advice that you can't agree with. There is a point at which parents must take a stand and follow the road less traveled.

This book is a tool for dealing effectively with crises and difficult situations. But remember no matter what you do, someone will disagree with you. Your mission, and you must accept it, is to be willing to take a stand, even when it is not popular, and navigate the stormy course of not having others agree.

CHAPTER TWO

CHOOSING A ROAD MAP:
EIGHT PRINCIPLES FOR MILITANT PARENTING

We need a road map in life if we are going to get anywhere. We may also need some guidelines to keep others from going somewhere we don't want them to go. In the amazing array of life's surprises, struggles, and necessary changes, the road is often unknown and rocky. *MILITANT PARENTING* offers some guidelines and principles which may help. It will no doubt be necessary for you to adapt its general guidelines to meet the situations which arise in your own community and family.

We all must choose some code, moral base, commandment, or philosophy to guide our children. At some point, however, we must step aside and they must find their own way. They alone will live with the consequences of their decisions. We are powerless in some areas to change them. As a rule, during adolescence their choices of friends (once they leave the house), driving habits, sexual behavior, and use of chemicals move more and more into their own realm of control.

The following are eight principles which I have found useful in raising my own kids and in my practice. Take some, and leave the rest, or ignore all of them. But give them some consideration. The point is to establish principles for yourself, convey them to your children, and then ultimately let your children take over for themselves, just as you did when you achieved independence from your parents.

PRINCIPLE#1: IT HURTS TO CHANGE.. IT HURTS NOT TO CHANGE.

You may experience feelings of guilt no matter which path you take. Staying stuck in unproductive parenting patterns can be as painful as not changing sometimes. Growth, however, often requires painful transitions. It is our nature to change and evolve. We are all here for some reason, and we must acknowledge that reason for our lives to have meaning. Our goal in raising our kids is to improve on the world we grew up in, just as we hope they will try to improve on their world.

Let's say you have a six-year old who throws a violent tantrum when he doesn't get what he wants in a grocery store. In one such instance recently, a mother slapped the child in the face. She was arrested for child abuse! And rightly so. Here's a woman whose parenting technique demands modification. No doubt she will find changing her current coping technique a challenge, but she would be well advised to deal with this challenge now rather than face a violent sixteen-year old ten years from now.

One way to understand the issue of change is to study the chronic slot machine user. If a slot machine paid off every fifth time or every seventh time, it would be boring and predictable. Instead it pays off randomly. This is known as _intermittent reinforcement_. Behavioral psychologists have known for decades that this learning pattern in which the recipient receives payoffs only occasionally, and according to no predictable pattern, provides the most lasting and intense desire to repeat a behavior.

The tantrum-throwing kid subconsciously knows

this. His behavior may pay off right away, or it may not. But you can be assured it <u>has</u> paid off in the past or he would not be repeating the behavior. Mom must either take the kid out of the store or allow him to throw the tantrum and not provide the pay off. <u>It will take a long time to change the behavior,</u> and plenty of shoppers will regard her with disdain. Still, this approach is far better than dealing with an out-of-control teenager or risking a jailed parent.

It is a normal behavior to resist change. The Militant Parent is willing to endure the wrath of the child or others in order to move the child toward more acceptable behavior.

PRINCIPLE #2: THINK SMALL

Elephants don't bite. Ants do. A kid does not become a problem overnight, and his or her problem will not be solved overnight. Change and growth in school, spirituality, self- discipline, and relationships are all long, arduous processes which require patience and acceptance of the fact that many, if not most, of our victories will be small ones, and hard won at that.

I once worked with a family who had an out-of-control fourth grader. He was not performing in school, was well below grade level, and was experiencing authority problems. They worked on one problem at a time to change his behavior, first getting the kid to go to school on time, then praising him for his progress; then getting him to do his homework on time, then praising him for his progress.

When I left them, he was still a little behind in school and still having minor authority problems; however, his progress was measurable... a little at a time to get there, a little at a time to change.

If we expect to improve our children, we must understand that it will take a long course of consistent, dedicated effort. Then, they must take over where we left off.

The Militant Parent is one who is willing to move slowly if necessary to change behavior which may have taken years to develop. He or she is willing to move in the right direction whether the child or others approve or not.

PRINCIPLE #3: SCREW UPS GIVE US OPPORTUNITIES TO IMPROVE AND PROGRESS

God has a great sense of humor. To know we are in a comedy of life set in motion by forces we can not possibly understand is restorative and awinspiring. It is the realization that we actually have some control in this process which sidetracks some of us. Of course, there are some things we cannot control. Still, when things go wrong, they often go wrong for a good reason.

Even disappointments illustrate how much our attitudes have to do with our abilities to turn challenges into opportunities for positive rewards.

Consider the story of the eternal optimist child and the eternal pessimist. At Christmas, the parents of the pessimist filled the boys room with toys, but when they opened his door, they found him crying. When asked what was wrong, he replied, "In just a little while all these toys will break." They opened the room of their optimistic child which they had filled with horse manure. This kid was screaming with glee and laughing and throwing the contents of the room all over. When asked what was going on, this kid replied, "In all this horse manure, there has to be a pony somewhere!"

One person's manure is another person's fertilizer. It is our attitudes towards our circumstances and inevitable screw-ups that makes life tolerable. When we believe we can get something from life and that we will eventually benefit from our suffering, we can tolerate the process better. No matter what happens in my life, I always say to myself, "God did not bring me all this way to drop me on my head." Remember: The attitude we have about an event is as important or more important than the event itself.

A wonderful but painful-to-watch movie appeared on television about a kid who liked to run. Actually, he ran every day because he wet the bed and his mother put his urine-stained sheets out each afternoon for all to see to humiliate him. He would run home faster than the other kids because he was ashamed of his enuresis problem. Not only did the kid eventually outgrow the problem and confront his shaming mother, but he also became an Olympic runner and changed his life because of his response to his deep personal humiliation. Problems and screw-ups provide us with opportunities.

On Christmas day a number of years ago, I had gone down to a meadow to fly a plane I had received for Christmas. (My family had its priorities in the right place in my opinion.) We were living in a three-story house in a remote canyon then, and when my son and I walked back up to the house, he said, "Isn't that the van down there?" Yes, it was the van, at the bottom of a hill where it had rolled out of the driveway because I had not set the brake properly. It was lying on its back like a cockroach... dead. Several tow trucks and the fire department brought it up, and it sat on the roadside for one month until the insurance company could figure out what to do with it. They actually paid me $200 more than I had paid for it, as it had appreciated in value! I went out and bought what I had really wanted, and another screw-up turned into a blessing.

When the accident occurred, I remember saying to myself; "This is a perfect screw-up." My wife did not join me in this conclusion at the time and was under-standably upset at me, my attitude, and the situation. During the period between the accident and the outcome, I did not feel distress. The ability to think in these terms is a willing choice, and it must be learned, practiced, and appreciated. It is the same ability and choice we must make with the mistakes and screw-ups of our children.

What a man thinketh, so he is.

My editor told me an enlightening story about her bright son who thought he hated school and neglected to register for college one year. When the omission was discovered, it was too late even for late registration. He was given, instead, the "opportunity" to do manual labor with a family friend for a fairly good salary. After a few months of digging founda-tions and framing houses, he made a straight line for school, completed all his college, plus and M.B.A., and is now the successful VP of a thriving manufacturing company. His screw-up provided him with the lesson that he did not want to work the rest of his life with his hands and back.

Screw-ups offer both the parent and the child an opportunity to grow. The militant parent is one who is able to allow "opportunities" to occur without controlling, interfering, or taking responsibility, so that a child learns a natural lesson in life. These opportunities range from falling off training wheels when he is learning to ride a bike to going to jail for not paying a traffic ticket. Each results in a lesson that must be learned, despite the pain involved.

PRINCIPLE #4: WE ARE MORE POWERFUL WHEN WE REALIZE WE ARE POWERLESS.

Some people will not or cannot change. We cannot change everything in our lives. To know which battles to fight and which battles to retreat from is part of surviving parenting. Some people would stand in front of a speeding ten-ton truck and expect not to get run down. This is not possible. It is also not possible to stop the direction of some headstrong people when they are determined to do something. Such a statement is, of course, age-specific, and does not apply to very small children. At some point, however, when the kid is six inches taller than you, has been-bench pressing 250 lbs. on a regular basis, and eats raw meat for breakfast, you may be in a position to admit you are powerless to physically control him. Better to call in rein-forcements or judiciously win by not going to battle where no victory is possible.

Take the case of a kid who decides to marry out of the "approval range" of her family. For whatever reasons, race, education, family background, or former experience, parents have traditionally claimed the right to approve or disapprove potential spouses for their sons and daughters. Some children will marry whomever they want when they turn 18. Some kids will mate with whomever they want, even if they are not 18. We cannot stop them. If we try, we sometimes do more to push them toward the inappro-priate mate than if we reasoned with them, told them the truth about our feelings, and then set them free to do what they feel they need to do.

One of my daughters married a young man my wife and I were reluctant to accept as a suitable partner. It was not because he was of a different culture. It was not because she was not ready to take

on the responsibility of marriage. It was because he
was violent and became physically abusive toward
her whenever he was angry.

My wife and I, as well as her brothers and sisters,
tried everything to encourage her not to return to
him after violent episodes. She would not listen.
Finally we gave up after a number of attempted inter-
ventions. Then she gave up too, and she was able to
end a rocky and painful relationship. Nothing we
said made it happen. When we stepped completely
out of it, she came to her own realization.

In the many years I served as a Deputy Probation
Officer, I worked with countless kids who ran away.
While I saw countless parents try to persuade their
teenagers to come home, it was often only after they
gave up trying that the kids would return.

There is a Tao saying:

SEEK NO CONTACT, AND YOU WILL HAVE UNION.

---

*Militant Parents learn when not to interfere. Accepting their
powerlessness, they develop strategies for staying out of
issues which are beyond their control, even though their
children or others may criticize them.*

PRINCIPLE# 5:   LEARN THAT IN CONFLICT, THE OTHER SIDE NEED NOT BE VIEWED AS WRONG

If I could give the world a gift, it would be an
understanding of this not-so-simple principle.
Conflict between people is based on the false belief
that for us to be right, the other side must be wrong.
Different _is_ _not_ _necessarily_ _wrong_.

Henry Kissinger was quoted as saying about the Mid-East crisis, "The greatest tragedy in the world is not when right *versus* wrong; It is when right versus right." We continually place people who do not agree with us in the camp of wrong. They are not always wrong, they are sometimes just different. We are _all_ different and might very well learn to be happy about it. It would be a boring world without differences.

To see Catholics, Mormons, Jehovah's Witnesses, Seventh-Day Adventists, Moslems, and Jews as all being "right" is beyond the comprehension of many people. Nationalities, religions, and ethnic groups often claim rightness for their camp and theirs alone. I believe we have a moral responsibility to attempt to instill our beliefs in our children. Let us not forget, however, that it is they and not we who will live out the rest of their lives (and possible time beyond) with the consequences of their moral decisions. We do not go to hell or purgatory or the Garden of Allah because of what they do. _We_ go because of what _we_ do.

We are much more likely to have children who are won over to our thinking when we honor their differences as they evolve. I know some of you will have trouble with this one, but here is reality in a nutshell. You must form values for yourself and I must do so for myself. Our children at some point must learn to make decisions for themselves. We must accept that their choices may be different from the choices we might make for them.

To be Militant Parents, we must resist labeling others as wrong because they differ in thought and practice from ourselves. As children grow up, we must accept and support their right to be different from us.

PRINCIPLE# 6: GROWING UP TAKES A LIFETIME, AND THE WORST THING YOU CAN DO IS ARRIVE

There is nothing more boring than trying to relate to someone who never questions, laughs at life, or accepts that he or she might have made a mistake. The rigidity of adulthood is not unique to the elderly. In fact, there are many elderly people who remain open, spontaneous, and continue to learn throughout their lifetimes. There are also teenagers who pass into rigid periods during which we cannot reason with them or teach them anything. They know it all.

I recall one of my daughters passing through this period and hearing her long diatribe about the value and essence of the punk music movement. I listened, she preached. Listening was the most judicious thing I could do, for to argue the point would have been of no value. She was passing through a stage toward adulthood and needed to argue about anything and everything. She eventually changed tastes, however, and remained open to other views, which has become the pattern of her life. The most important thing is that she was not provoked to become rigid at this period in her life as so many people are.

Self-discipline is an invaluable quality in all of us. When I can get parents to stop obsessing over their children, I find that they have issues in themselves which they also want to resolve. Most of us have enough to do to improve ourselves to keep us busy for the rest of our lives. We can probably help our children more by modeling change, commitment, and self-discipline than by trying to meddle in areas of their lives which are none of our business. It takes some people a lifetime to achieve self-discipline. Some people never get it.

Militant Parents realize that their children will be growing throughout their lifetimes. They know this because they respect growth in themselves as well. Taking on responsibility is a process and not an event.

PRINCIPLE#7: CONFRONTATION IS AN ACT OF GRACE

The most important people in our lives are the ones who are honest with us. We often remember the people who tell us the painful truth, but who do not have an agenda which dictates how we or others must change. Militant Parents learn how to initiate confrontation without creating hostility. They are willing to confront, but they are also willing to leave things in a child's hands whether he changes or not.

Good teachers, counselors, and parents understand this aspect of helping people to change. They particularly understand this when a person is resistant to change. Change is better offered as an option, not a requirement. Some people prefer to stay stuck in a life dilemma instead of following through completely with a needed change. Nine-tenths of a decision will leave them feeling crazy; to make a complete commitment to change would eventually render them sane. It is not necessary for us to feel the pain an undecided person is having to be able to assist him. In fact, it may increase his burden.

Parents are in a difficult position with their kids. They can tell kids the truth as they see it, and then allow them to do whatever they want to do in response to their suggestions. They can also be authoritarian and risk breaking the child's spirit. The choices here must be made on a situation-by-situation basis. A parent may wish to stop a kid or hold him accountable for the destruction of the parents' property and yet allow the kid to take

apart his own property to "fix it," allowing the kid
the wisdom that comes from such an experience.
For example, a teenager may be held financially
accountable for a broken door or hole in the wall
made during a moment of rage, but he may be
allowed to "work on his car" and live with the
consequences of taking it apart should it become
inoperable as a result.

Again, this is all age-specific, and it is not optional
to allow a child to run out in the street when he is
three years old. As a child gets older, his options
increase. Here are some acceptable confrontational
comments parents may wish to file away for future
reference:

- ☹ It is unpleasant to see you eat with your
  mouth open.
- ☹ You have bad breath, and you need to brush
  your teeth.
- ☹ You need a bath; you smell like phys-ed.
- ☹ I am not willing to loan you money because
  you didn't repay the last debt.
- ☹ I am not willing to indulge you by buying
  special foods you like or doing the wash
  until you show a willingness to treat me
  with decency and respect.

And my personal favorite: No, you cannot borrow
the car because the last time you did, you brought it
back without any gas in it and slimed the front seat
with whatever major food group you were ingesting.

---

*The Militant Parent is willing to expose the truth when
necessary, even if the truth will temporarily hurt someone
else's feelings. Often growth does not occur without some
pain preceding it. He or she understands that confrontation
can be an act of grace.*

PRINCIPLE #8:   KEEP A SENSE OF HUMOR

One of the greatest gifts parents must cultivate is a sense of humor. Families supply us with never-ending reasons for laughter. While we cannot laugh at everything, the more humor we can find in our challenges as parents, the better.

I tell my kids regularly, "Always remember one thing." When they ask "What?" I say, "It does not matter what it is, just always remember one thing."

Just last week, in an effort to discharge family secrets in a spirit of complete openness, I went to each of my four children and confessed to them that I was not their real mother.

Militant Parents can laugh at themselves and laugh at the foibles of their children. They see laughter as a source of joy and not as an alternative to working on a situation. They sense the problem will eventually pass and can see humor in much of what life brings.

CHAPTER THREE

JB'S SEVEN RULES FOR SURVIVAL

At the turn of the century, children were sent away from home at about the time they entered puberty, which is still the practice in many countries today. A variety of options provided a pressure valve and a clearer transition to adulthood. Girls would be sent to a finishing school if the family had financial resources. Boys might enter an apprenticeship with a master in a trade or craft who could teach them their future livelihood. Some girls worked as "nannies" for well-to-do families. Often young adults moved a short distance from home and began lives of their own with a marriage partner. The point is that they achieved separation from the primary family unit, at least by a little distance.

In J.R.R. Tolkien's "LORD OF THE RINGS," Bilbo Baggins lives in a little hamlet which identifies teenagers as passing from childhood to adulthood at 32 years old! While this may have seemed preposter-ous at the time (1939), it is often not far from reality in our culture today. We lack those *Rites Of Passage* which help us identify when a child graduates from childhood to adulthood. Where is this line of passage? Is it bar mitzvah? Graduation from college? Gang initiations? Driving? Drinking? Voting? Turning 18? Childbirth?

The rituals some cultures cling to allow everyone to identify a young person's change in status from one maturity level to another. The vague, drawn-out process of achieving adulthood in our culture means that no one knows for certain what to expect from a child during this poorly delineated passage from childhood to adulthood. Cultural anthropologists

have identified the word A<small>BRAXAS</small>. It means to
progress from childhood to adulthood in the eyes of
the tribe. We have no such word in our culture.

Instead, we maintain this twilight zone of age warp
we call the "teens" which seems to stretch from eleven-
teen or twelveteen to twentyteen or twenty-oneteen.

We even have some laws which contribute to this
absurdity:

When children are 16, they can drive with parental
permission.

If children are legally emancipated from the parent, they
can sign contracts, but only if they have the legal status of
emancipation first.

If children are 17, with parental permission, they can
serve in the military, die for their country, but not buy
alcohol in many states until they are 21 years old. (Unless
it's on a military base).

If children commit crimes past the age of 14, but are not
yet 18, they can be remanded to the adult court, at which
time they may be placed in the California Youth
Authority. The severity of CYA punishment places them
in the same unsatisfactory atmosphere as an adult
incarcerated for a similar crime.

We tell children under the age of 18 that they cannot
smoke, then make cigarettes readily available and flood
the media with images showing smoking as sophisticated.

Then, to add insult to injury, we tell them, "Y<small>OU'RE TOO</small>
<small>YOUNG FOR PHYSICAL INTIMACY. BESIDES, SEX IS DIRTY.</small>
<small>SAVE IT FOR THE ONE YOU LOVE.</small>"

Confused? Well <u>they</u> are. And if we're honest with ourselves, so are we. We live in a society which generates laws in a bewildering and fluffy manner. No wonder that as parents we experience self-doubt and stress. How does the Militant Parent arm himself or herself against the slings and arrows of outrageous ambiguity? You may wish to memorize and internalize the maxims below.

JB's RULE #1: THE KID DID NOT COME WITH DIRECTIONS.

OK, this may sound a little far out to some of you, but think again. What does the average person with no training in the kidology department know about childrearing? You can read a book. You can follow your parents' guidelines, which might work if your spouse agrees. You can follow the guidelines of your spouse, but they might not work for you. Whose advice will you follow? See what I mean? We often run around without a map, trying to find our way to a place we have never been while we resent those around us who do not expect to arrive at the same mysterious destination. Remember, a kid does not come with directions. If one did, he or she would probably grow up resembling the time clock on your VCR which constantly blinks because you have not programmed it correctly. Many times we are clueless about what is going on in a child's mind and soul, and after all, children are not born clutching a list of instructions.

In the world of parenting, we sometimes have to make it up as we go and besides, each kid is different! Some kids gravitate toward acceptable behavior so easily it takes no effort whatsoever to raise them. Some are high maintenance. They come to us this way right from the beginning and sometimes stay that way all their lives, no matter what we do.

High maintenance kids experience one crisis after another as they grow up. They require resources and limits, and sometimes bring us heartaches few folks even dream of. They do grow up, however. Sometimes it's sooner; too often it's later.

Here are a few humorous suggestions related to the frustrations of parenthood I have collected over the years.

> *"I'll send you right back where you came from and make another one."*   Bill Cosby

> *It's never too late to consider retroactive birth control.*
>   *Anonymous optimist*

> *Teenagers should be freeze-dried at 13 and thawed out when they are 24.*

> *Or...Parents of teenagers should be freeze dried and thawed out when their youngest child reaches 24. (Anonymous optimist with even sketchier background in the biological sciences.)*

AND MY ALL-TIME-PERSONAL FAVORITE:
Living with teenagers is like being bitten to death by ducks.

JB'S RULE #2: FLUFFY LIMITS WILL YIELD YOU FLUFFY RESULTS

This rule applies to both kids and adults. We are, to an extent, in our current muddle because we do not provide consistent, clear-cut rules for our teenagers when they pass into this transitional era of their lives.

The old rules they understood as children cease to apply. The freedoms (and responsibilities) they will later face as adults are not yet available either.

Often, they truly do not understand what rules apply to them; and, just as often, we don't either. Doesn't someone have to set the rules? Yes! When no one does this judiciously and consistently, everyone remains confused. We then sometimes follow this lack of guidance by criticizing kids for not living up to expectations we never told them we had. Rules are good. Rules provide multiple types of safety.

My editor told me an inspiring story about one of her professors, Dr. Molly Mason Brown of Scripps College, former director of Claremont's Mary B. Eyre Nursery School.

When the un-fluffy, limit-setting Dr. Brown's children were young, she trained them to respond instantly to her direction whenever she spoke to them in a serious tone of voice. She rarely used this voice to obtain their attention and obedience, but when she did, the children knew she meant business.

One day the family was in the foothills of San Bernardino picnicking. Only a few miles away was a field where pilots who flew gliders landed their planes. On this day, the children were playing on a hillside meadow when a full-size manned glider suddenly lost altitude and came right at them from behind. Dr. Brown looked up to see the plane descending and calmly and quickly commanded, "Down," motioning with her hands for them to drop flat on the ground. All three children did so instantaneously and were thus saved from catastrophe.

Sex provides us with an excellent example of our fluffy thinking. Schools are regularly requested by parents not to offer sex education. Churches say, "Leave the job to the parents." Often, children fail to get adequate, accurate, un-fluffy information from their parents, so no one does the job right. The result: Children are poorly prepared to deal with the pressures and problems of a culture whose overt and covert message mercilessly propels them toward sexual activity as early as their pre-teen years.

Everyone blames everyone else, and no one accepts the responsibility. The sad consequence is a generation of young people who Think they know all they need to know about sex but are actually quite ignorant. Even more unfortunate is the tragedy of kids who are not fully informed about sexually-transmitted diseases, the ease with which women get pregnant, and the calamity of entering into sexual relationships without the benefit of maturity and the lifetime commitment involved in marriage.

A number of years ago I tried an illuminating experiment with teenagers who were hospitalized for chemical dependency treatment. For approximately two years, I conducted a sex information group with these teenagers. One might have expected that they would be well informed, since their lifestyles lay at the outer edge of experimentation regarding many types of defiant behaviors. Unfortunately, in a situation which encouraged them to ask and then answer questions anonymously, they showed themselves to be far from adequately informed. When it came to sexually-transmitted diseases, birth control, and sound medical information about their bodies, these kids were a disaster.

We know after studying many educational models that adequate information is critically important in assisting young people to avoid the pitfalls of early sexual problems such as pregnancy, inappropriate attachments, and sexually- transmitted diseases. What does work to un-fluff the topic of sexuality is to answer questions frankly when they come up as the child grows. Additionally, we must make well-chosen, illustrated books available which will help kids access the most current and useful information. (It is surprising how motivated kids are to read when they really want the information.) There are numerous fine books available which deal openly and honestly with this subject matter. If you need guidance, consult your family doctor or pediatrician.

This brings us to the second rule.

JB's RULE #3: INFORMATION IS POWER; ALTERNATIVES ARE POWER.

Sometimes we become immobilized in parenting because we do not know or can't decide what to do. We do not completely understand how to live with a teenager or adult child who refuses to grow up. We muddle through, isolated, scared, blaming ourselves or our partners for our children's failings and disasters.

Take the mom and dad who are told that their son is below grade level in reading and spelling. They lament, "Where did we go wrong?" Worried about the future and the non-accomplishment of their child, they take it out on the kid, themselves, the teacher, the school, or each other. The fact is, all kids do not advance academically at the same pace. Some are slower and some are faster. If a kid is behind his class, it does not always mean that his or her future academic career is in serious jeopardy. Take heart. To solve problems, know your options and consider some alternatives:

✔ Hire a competent tutor a few years older than the kid for a lot less money than you would pay a professional. (Unless you have the financial resources.) Then allow the tutor and tutoree to spend time after the lesson having fun .

✔ Tell the kid what you are proud of in his or her accomplishments and do not focus only on the negative.

✔ Tell the kid how you overcame academic challenges when you were growing up. Do not, however, compare your accomplishments or the accomplishments of siblings to the kid's! He or she is a different person in a different situation.

✔ Remind the kid that your involvement in this situation is because you love and care about him or her and that a major goal in your life is to do all you can to help each member of the family prepare for a suitable and useful life.

We need choices. We need to know and examine alternatives that have worked for others. This doesn't mean we will do exactly what another person did, but it provides us with inspiration.

When you flip through a parenting magazine, it offers no articles about living with the teenager from hell. Parenting magazines sell diapers and baby formula to people who are not yet fearing that their well-ordered lives, as they may know them, may turn to chaos when their teenagers lurch into the world of raging hormones, blue hair, and earrings dangling from their noses. This is when parents discover the truth in the African saying that it takes a village to raise a child. Villages offer options beyond those which a single parent or pair of parents can make available.

Many American communities provide Little League, Girl Scouts, community service opportunities, and church groups for young people. Not all kids gravitate willingly toward these organizations. Some

will still prefer to hang out in parks, or drink, or dye
their hair blue, or shave their heads in alluring
geometric patterns. It is important to remember that
all the kids who dress or style their hair in a certain
current fashion are not headed down a path to
disaster. This period of revolt may, however, be
extremely distressing for the adults in the kids' lives.
Our power as parents is to realize that they will no
doubt have all this worked out 20 years from now. We
have only to survive the "stage" the kid is going
through. After three decades of working with kids
and their parents, I have seen most of the kids
outgrow most of their problems. Which is not to say it
isn't a living hell for parents while they are doing so.

---

*Know your options, consider your best alternatives, and rely
on community resources for information and support as
necessary.*

JB's RULE #4: WHEN YOU HAVE A NUMBER OF PUPPIES, SOME OF THEM WILL PEE ON YOUR RUG.

Do you have a poltergeist in your house? A ghost
often inhabits a household with more than one child
in it. It's a curious thing about lodging more than one
child: Things just happen in the house, and no one
knows how or why they took place! I pity kids with
no siblings. They can't blame much on the dog,
because dogs generally don't party when their
masters are away. "Things" will happen when you
have children. Damage will occasionally occur to
your property, not because they are bad kids, but
because they are just kids. A reasonable way to
minimize this eventuality is to encourage as much
honesty as possible when the kids are young,
rewarding their instances of exemplary behavior and
their responsible, up-front acceptance for mistakes
when they occur.

Lying to parents is sometimes equated in a child's mind to survival. If the kid tells the truth, he sometimes fears he or she will get in more trouble than if he lies. Parents need to condition children to think the other way around.

A reasonable option here is for kids to have One Free Everything (with extreme behavior excluded), which means you accept the fact that they may screw up at least once and should be forgiven. We have a criminal justice system which works this way, and many persons are diverted from disaster by the careful handling of their first offense. After that, more serious consequences must occur.

For some kids, feeling guilty about their bad behavior is sufficient to keep it from reoccurring. Others need more pain to internalize the message. Children, like puppies, do not all respond to the same rewards and punishments. But every dog trainer I've met with believes that puppies handled with firmness and affection turned out the better and more reliable companions than animals whose spirits have been broken by excessive and inconsistent punishment. Reward rather than punishment is a far better way to shape behavior. It is possible to verbally praise a kid for accepting responsibility and still give conse- quences for the unacceptable act if necessary.

JB'S RULE #5: TEENAGERS TODAY ARE NOT AS BAD AS YOU SUSPECT.

Are you outraged by the behavior of your teenager? Do you think he or she has been perma- nently damaged by the effects of television on his or her sponge-like brain? Well, here's an important news brief: Teenagers today are not as bad as you think.

Generations of parents since the beginning of time have been outraged by the appalling behavior of the next generation. Remember, it is this generation's job to offend adults. If they do not offend or at least challenge their elders, there is no movement through that stage of breaking away which no one can define, no one knows how to label, and no one can identify as to its beginning or end.

Literature is peppered with the typical rebellions of teenagers: Absolom, Antigone, Romeo and Juliet, Tom Jones and Huck Finn. All represent young people who broke from the traditions of their parents or guardians. Like the prodigal son in the Bible, many children disappoint the significant adults in their lives, only to return later to those who continued to love them. After their return, most of them live out a life of love and family loyalty and all is well.

Another example of this classic need to revolt is humorously presented in the lyrics of Meredith Wilson's

"The Music Man"

★ "Does your son rebuckle his knickerbockers below his knees"?

★ "Is he starting to use words like "swell" and "so'z your old man"?

★ "Is there a dime novel hidden in the corn-crib"?

"You know why? It's because there is a pool hall. Yes, right here in River City"!

★ Later, in the 20s the problem was flappers and the scandalous dance they performed. Surely the Charleston would lead the country to ruin.

★ Then came the swing bands. More scandalous. (Most people were unaware that in Vienna in the 1800s riots broke out when the waltz was first introduced.)

★ Later still, came Elvis...with adolescent girls passing out at the mere sight of his wildly gyrating hips.

★ Still later, we survived the Beatles, whom most adults at the time thought should be exterminated with bug spray.

★ Then there was disco, then punk, heavy metal...and like the Energizer Bunny, the revolt against what is considered acceptable and respectable, keeps going and going and going.

Every generation adopts a music, dress, hair, and language style which runs counter to mainstream culture. Don't forget, It is supposed to offend someone All the better if it happens to be parents and other easily shocked authority figures in the kid's life.

One of the funniest things I have observed in the current generation is its need to cut off hair to go counter to the preference of the last generation, which grew it long. What kids accept as cool goes in cycles. Flow with it and it's a lot more fun. And relax. Almost invariably they will have it all worked out by their wedding night.

I worked with a warm and loving family a number of years ago who, in spite of being open and flexible about most matters, had an ongoing agenda for their son's hair. Cut it. He didn't. They persisted. He went off to college and still didn't. They continued to persist. Finally, he graduated from college and they gave up. Then he cut his hair. Sound familiar? This little circular dance is repeated in countless scenarios with our children. Remember the admonition from the Mother Goose's nursery rhymes: "Leave them alone, and they'll come home, wagging their tails behind them." In many cases, Mom Goose still knows best. If it's not going to matter in 50 years, don't sweat it.

While one of my sons was going to college, he died his hair orange. Nice touch. He looked like an advertisement for an inferior hair product that should never have gained approval from the F.D.A. My wife (who was much more tolerant than me) and I decided to mind our own business. He graduated. His hair grew out. The world did not come to an end. Interesting how these minor domestic crises pass. Especially when we don't do anything aggressive about them.

Psychiatrists and psychologist have studied teenagers worldwide for some time, and much to our surprise, we are convinced that teenagers are healthier than they have ever been throughout history. Two researchers, Offer and Offer, have noted across many diverse populations of teenagers, both within the United States and around the world, that the majority of teenagers (approximately 80%) do not experience significant psychological disturbance. By and large they show good coping skills and achieve a smooth transition as they progress into adulthood. (For more discussion of this you may wish to consult Child and Adolescent Psychiatry: A Comprehensive Textbook, edited by Melvin Lewis.)

Normal teenagers (whoever they are) may not resemble the same teenagers or young adults you must deal with. Just keep in mind that teenagers feel obligated to come up with novel ways to offend adults. This is part of their job description. Our kids are not all normal. But then, we are not all normal either. What is important to note here is that most

kids will pass through insurrection to emerge as
stable, productive adults. But, oh, the pain of the
journey in getting there.

What is not all right is when your child ventures
into the permanent damage zones and risks untreat-
able sexually-transmitted diseases, permanent brain
damage from drugs and alcohol, and serious conflicts
with the law. Because of the seriousness of these
problems, the militant parent must arm for battle.
Again, it is important to keep in mind that most kids
pass through this experimental stage in their develop-
ment without incurring lasting damage with very few
exceptions.

JB's RULE #6: WITH VERY FEW EXCEPTIONS KIDS ARE NOT THE WAY THEY ARE BECAUSE THEY FELL ON THEIR HANDS WHEN THEY WERE TWO.

We all fall into the trap of inventing some clinical
or physical reason for why our kid is not OK. Listen
to a few of the more popular reasons:

★ He was born under the wrong sign.

★ She is just like her mother; he is just like his father.

★ It's the schools these days (unless you're the teacher, and then it's the parents).

★ It is the influence of the drug culture.

★ There is violence and sex on television.

And of course, my personal preference: "He/she fell
on his/her head when he/she was two".

All children fall on their heads when they are two.
They are top-heavy and still unaware that they are
subject to gravity.

Most children have some problem to overcome in their lives. We are all too ready to provide ourselves and them with some excuse for why they experience difficulties. Perhaps this is because we fear that they are incapable of dealing with life on life's terms. Life is difficult, and then you die. The tragedy is that when some people think that their children or they themselves create or deserve impending doom, no one in this insidious morass of defeatism ever attempts anything worthwhile or demanding. We can overcome adversity. Adversity is the catalyst that motivates great people to become great.

I once worked with a family to whom I was trying to point out the successes they had already achieved with their five-year old son. I said, "I'll bet he doesn't go to the bathroom in the middle of the room." They countered with, "No, but he does go to the bathroom in the corner!" When I inquired as to why this might be occurring, they gave me a long explanation about a trip the boy had taken to his natural mother's house one weekend several years before. They insisted that he had not been the same since. They did not realize that the child was fully capable of stopping the objection-able behavior. Nor did they see that they were also capable of stopping the behavior from reoccurring.

After considering the child's successes they could understand and build on, they realized that the boy was capable and began to reassert their authority with him. Yes, he did get fully toilet trained and no longer peed in the corner, in the middle of the room, or anywhere inappropriate. What was important here was not that they had to enter therapy to do the job of changing the boy's behavior. What was important was that they had to realize they were capable of doing the job themselves.

A few years ago I was speaking to friends at a party about my struggles to climb Mt. Whitney, a formidable 14,495 foot ascent. My excuse for not reaching the top in my first attempt was the wrong gear. On another attempt it was not enough time. My final assault was successful, but resulted in a world-class headache and extreme nausea due to altitude sickness. After I had told my story, the wife of a friend informed me that her husband had reached the summit three times. Most people would have been duly impressed, but I knew that her husband had suffered from polio as a child, had weakened ankle muscles, needed two canes, and walked with great pain every day of his life. My eyes still tear up when I contemplate the courage of this hero who, during his entire life, let nothing stand in the way of his achieving his dreams.

Because I work in the world of recovery from chemical dependency, I operate with a keen realization of the handicaps in people's lives. Over and over I see that it is the handicaps that people can't see that they find most difficult to deal with. Their hidden wounds leave them convinced that they are different from their fellow men and women. We are not all created equal, but we have to move forward with the things God gave us. We must work with the limitations and abilities unique to us. The worst thing we can do is to tell our children that they are not capable. Worse yet is when parents believe that they cannot confidently set defensible limits or deal effectively with a child who is determined to blame them for their woes. We are all far more resilient and capable than we realize. Our children are also capable. We must learn to trust in ourselves and others. In many of the painful situations which emerge in our lives, the situation may get worse before it gets better. But it does get better. Throughout life, as in nature, there is a welcome calm after the storm. Our lives and our children's lives are no exception.

Open And Closed Family Systems

Some family systems are Closed Systems, which means that no information gets out of the family and no information gets in. Others are Open Systems which allow for information to flow out and in. In these systems, there are no secrets. This is not to say that sensitive matters concerning the family need to be published in the newspaper, but the information can be shared with persons outside the family. Members of such families are allowed to grow when new alternatives are offered. Openness is the basis and strength of support organizations like Tough Love, Alanon, Families Anonymous, and many groups which are made up of friends who meet informally with one another to tell the truth instead of distorting it.

We Are Only As Sick As Our Secrets

The expression of secrets can be healing. When we observe some cultures, we can see that there is great pressure on members of the family not to bring shame or disgrace to the family. Asain cultures are clearly affected by this pressure. We sometimes fail to realize that our culture places similar pressure on the members of families. We are pressured to disguise vulnerabilities within the family, and we feel compelled to not share information that would make the world judge us harshly. The problem is that such pressure sometimes creates isolation of the family or members of the families, and it further encourages distortions of the truth, distortion of feelings, and ultimately further isolation and mental instability.

Family Secrets

It is almost never the family secret alone that is the problem in a dysfunctional family. All families have secrets. It is the enormous effort and destruction of honesty and trust that it takes to protect the secret that creates dysfunction. Please read the following and memorize it if you can. It will offer you the same important lessons it has taught me:

When a major caretaker has a secret, and the caretaker does not deal with the secret, the child will act out the secret even if the child does not know what the secret is.

Let me give you an example. I worked with a intelligent young man one time who had been caught shoplifting. He was a good kid in general, but his parents were understandably disturbed at his behavior. The father was a doctor who was extremely respectable. When I told the family about the need children had to act out the secrets of their parents, the father openly admitted to his family that he habitually stole small parts, tools, screws, and other marginally inexpensive items every time he went into a hardware store. Part of the healing of the boy was the father's willingness to admit and then change his behavior.

The Bible puts it in these terms:

The sins of the fathers will be visited unto the children for seven generations.

It doesn't say "inflicted on"; it says Visited. Not all visitors in our lives are permanent. We can do something about the family sins and secrets by blowing the cover on the lies and deception. Everyone knows something about the family scandals anyway. We all carry the shame, even if we don't discuss it.

JB's Rule #7: God did not offer me an internship

Our children are the children of God and live in a world which we may never completely comprehend. We cannot walk in their shoes and should not try. We would no doubt give them athlete's foot. We must accept that they are on a journey which is not ours. The difficulty in this lies in the pain we experience while watching them do things differently from the ways we think things should be done. It is painful to watch someone you love fail. However, failure is a door through which we gain wisdom. Wisdom does not always come from the experience of others; often it comes from our own heartbreak and insight, as a direct result of our own mistakes.

In my family of origin, no one went to college. In fact, I was the only one to graduate from high school! During much of my childhood, my mother and stepfather told me I should seriously consider working with my hands because my academic skills were so poor. After earning a bachelor's degree, master's degree, and now a doctoral degree, I have decided they were wrong. We are all capable of accomplishments when we try. To tell children they are not capable of achievement is the cruelest and most destructive thing we can do to them. No one knows the capabilities of the human spirit better than those who have been told that they cannot do something and have gone on to achieve success in spite of their personal prophets of doom.

The other bog of this judgmental sump hole relates to telling children that they are Not working up to their Full Potential.. I suspect this line is engraved on many school teachers' and parents' brains much the same way that graffiti used to clutter up walls until we learned we could take it off and keep it off. Who does work up to his or her full potential? I don't always, and you probably don't either. Now that this little secret is out, let's not expect our children to do anything we or others are not capable of. I do not recall ever hearing a teacher, tutor, or parent say, "I think this child is working up to his full potential."

Doesn't it seem incredible that every child is failing in this seemingly critical arena where a basically unmeasurable commodity or potential is being assessed by persons who are potentially in many cases untrained in psychological evaluation? Is it that they have a need to blame a child's shortcomings on someone other than themselves? Perhaps we have all fallen victim to the overuse of the "P" word..Potential. It is not potential that makes the difference; it is the discipline and drive each person has to maximize whatever gifts he or she is handed in life that makes the difference.

The most critical issue in education is whether or not children master the skills appropriate to facilitate continued learning. Can they read at grade level? Can they do math? Can they articulate what they need to say on paper and through spoken words? Do they get along with their peers most of the time? Can they challenge an adult in a socially acceptable manner when they disagree? If not, provide them with skill training. Does anyone ask you, Mr. Dad, what grade you got in high school algebra? How about you, Ms. Mom? Does your boss really care whether you got a C or a D in high school history? Also of critical concern today is the fact that while many kids are staying in school, some of them cannot read or do simple math when they graduate. It is the operational skill level of our kids that will eventually make the difference in how they do in the world. For the record, no study has ever determined a significant relationship between a person's high school and college grades and his or her success in a chosen profession.

When I teach at colleges and universities, I constantly remind students who want to become counselors and therapists that no patient will ever ask them what grade they earned in a family counseling class or any other class for that matter. Who cares? What is important is that the student develops the skill level to handle the job.

Some kids need to flop around on land before they find their way back to the water. They started in water. They will make it... probably. If they don't, they must shoulder the responsibility for their failure. If they do, they deserve the credit for their success. If no responsibility is accepted, you will be dealing with one very immature adult. If you take too much responsibility, you will be one very unhappy and guilt-ridden parent. In worst-case scenarios there are those areas of foggy responsibility in which the child and parent vacillate between blaming first themselves and then the other, never attacking and/or eliminating the problem. The result resembles a volleyball game in which two players allow the ball to fall between them, after which each blames the other.

Each of us is a child of God. God does not have grandchildren; He only has children. To know the fate or outcome of a life is beyond us, and to attempt to take on such an unrealistic responsibility is to rob others of their dignity and burden ourselves with issues beyond our control. We are all children, and we are in His hands. Sometimes we must allow others the dignity to fail.

Chapter Four

GOOD GUYS AND BAD GUYS

We live in a "good-guy/bad-guy" culture. Our Puritan roots, our obsession with identifying good vs. evil, our attraction to cops and robbers, cowboys and Indians, and other polarities sets us all up to see black and white in every aspect of our lives. This tendency toward polarization is not, of course, original to our era. Herman Melville wrote an entire chapter in "Moby Dick" in which he expounded (with little scientific evidence) on the differences between black and white creatures of the various species.

Naturally, with an already deeply ingrained cultural consciousness of evil like this as part of our programming, we act out this same simplistic approach to perception when we engage in family problem solving. In fact, it often determines our style of parenting. One parent says:

"IF YOU CONTROL THESE KIDS MORE, THEY WILL BE A LOT EASIER TO LOVE."

The other parent says:

"IF YOU LOVE THESE KIDS MORE, THEY WILL BE A LOT EASIER TO CONTROL."

Because both statements are true, this is the classic impasse in divergent parenting. It is so classic that I now view it as Normal. It is normal because it so often focuses the fundamental power struggle in ordinary families. It is normal because more families experience this problem than not. (Normal is defined in our culture as reflecting a particular behavior that occurs in the majority of the population.)

We are faced here with the normal-dysfunctional situation vs. the abnormal-functional situation. To be functional in this model, parents must set out to navigate an abnormal course which would not be attempted by the majority of people. It is the task, however, of the Militant Parent to do just that. By trial and error, Militant Parents unite and commit to a course they can both follow in order to achieve consistency in dealing with their children.

I suspect that as many as 90% of American families live with some degree of the "good-guy/bad-guy" paradigm. Someday I will advertise a support group, Normal People Anonymous, for the few people who grew up in a family and can say, "If I didn't get the consequence from Dad, I would get it from Mom." There will be an 800 number to call, but no one will answer. Since you are reading this, you probably can't attend. I am starting the group, but in good conscience I can't attend either.

A united parental front is so rare that when I hear about it in a case history, I literally perch on the edge of my chair and listen with awe. In all the years I have been counseling, I have seen fewer than five situations in which the parents were completely united. The person who is the product of such a family is perplexed by the viewpoint of his or her dysfunctional mate and is equally baffled by the apparent dysfunction of the rest of the world. It's no longer easy to be well adjusted.

JB's Rule # 8: Do it wrong if you have to, but do it together

If you can figure out how to avoid all conflict in parenting, you will shock your kids (and probably the dog) so thoroughly that they will all think you have "gone around the bend." They won't know what hit them (not you, to be sure, just a figure of speech). Kids only have one masterful defense against the united front parenting technique: Make mom and dad feel guilty. Usually the good guy is more easily hooked by guilt. The bad guy is more adept at fending it off because he or she understands the guilt game a little better. The trick here is to join forces, at least in front of the kids, and refuse to let them play you off. They will still try. So will the dog and your in-laws.

People do not manipulate you because they are sick or perverse. It is normal for humans as well as animals to maneuver to get what they want. The dog knows which members of the family are serious and who is just "blowing smoke" and not likely to follow through.

I had a dog years ago that was always stretching when I came upstairs. I couldn't understand why she did this until one day I noticed our waterbed slowly sloshing. Mindy knew it wasn't OK to be on the bed, so she would jump down, stretch convincingly, and pretend she had been napping on the floor. My wife didn't mind if she was on the bed. The dog knew which one of us allowed it and which did not. If dogs are this insightful, imagine what kids pick up from our body language, facial expressions, and tones of voice.

Often when the Divide and Conquer problem surfaces, a second marriage is blamed for the problem. Two decades ago the primary reason for the breakup of a second marriage was generally identified as problems over kids. Now, conflict over children has been identified as the primary reason for the breakup of first marriages as well. Control in a second-marriage scenario is perceived by children as remaining the inalienable right of the natural parent. This conviction leads to critical conflicts during the parenting and step-parenting process.

STEP-PARENT GOOD-GUYS AND BAD-GUYS

The issue of whether or not an alternative parent has the right to parent extends well beyond the step-parent. School officials, teachers, and authority figures in the community are all adults whom children must learn to respect and obey. Granted, as adults we occasionally seriously question authority ourselves, but we have generally developed an ability to co-exist with authority so that we get along with minimal disruption in our lives.

The problem of control festers in kids who want to have their own way. They may also be trying to show that they are more valued than the alternative parent. When the parents and kid get caught up in this scenario, loyalty, love, and allegiance may be misinterpreted or acted out in destructive behaviors. Natural parents in a divorce or separation from the other natural parent suffer from the G-Word... Guilt. They often believe that the right to control a child's behavior should not be given to a parent other than the natural mother and father. They themselves often do not accept the control and limits which the estranged parent may try to impose on them.

The classic problem in divorce is that everyone acts out and revolts against the boundaries and limits which were formerly in place. This is literally what a divorce is... a breakdown of the boundaries and limits of the family. A marital relationship is not just a commitment; it is a series of commitments. In divorce, each person must develop new relationships which have new rules which can and will change. When we continue to hate and feel resentment for former spouses, they continue to live inside us "rent-free." This situation is intensified by the continual need to relate and/or wage war through the mutual children.

It is easy for either a natural parent or an alternative parent to loosen the limits and boundaries on the
kids, thereby causing a rift in leadership within the
family. Accusations, innuendo, and gossip all play a
part in the message to the kid that says, "I love you
and therefore I am always going to let you have your
way." Ironically, limit setting and enforcement of
simple disciplinary structures are often not
perceived as messages of love. It is easier to let kids
have their way in the short run than to set strict and
consistent limits. In the long run, it is the latter
which are more effective.

The new stepparent (or "friend," grandmother,
grandfather, or other adult living with the child) must
not only Own the right, they must Exercise the right
to set and enforce limits. When the natural parent
does not allow this, chaos follows. The kid will soon
be running the family. If the natural parent does not
facilitate the transition so that the new parent or
partner parents the children in the home, there will
be no control. This problem may be compounded by
the fear on all sides that this transferred control may
be abusive, arbitrary, or unloving. Unfortunately, this
is a possibility. It is also a possibility with natural
parents, and thus it becomes another of the factors
that explains why this process of transferring control
is so difficult and complex. Here are some key
questions adults must answer:

1. Do you and your new partner want to stay
   together after the children are raised? If so, you
   must band together on your approach to the kids.
   Robert Louis Stevenson said, "Children who are
   born of lovers are born orphan." That is the way
   it should be. The kids leave and the parents still
   have a life together.
2. Are you both willing to read, go to parent
   training, or seek counseling to work through the

difficult transitions? If so, you will stand a better chance of surviving this difficult transition.

3. Are both of you willing to face the reality that if multiple children are involved from several marriages, the limits and rules may not be the same for all the children? If so, you will be better off because you are seeing the world as it really is. If you want fair, you must go to Pomona. (Note: This is a regional joke, as Pomona is the seat of the county fair.) Total fairness in life is an illusion, often perpetuated by kids who want their parents to feel guilty and obligated to give them what they want. Working toward fairness with kids is an ideal, but in reality, with two or more homes and two or more sets of parents to deal with, a blended family will not always achieve perfect consis-tency. Work toward improvement, not perfection.

Very young children accept changes in authority easier than teenagers, who may deeply resent the intrusion of the new adult into the family. If you are embarking on this new transition, remember that teenagers generally resent the control of the natural parents as well. The war you may have to fight is not solely the result of the divorce. It is often the natural consequence of a child entering the mental state the Germans call sturm und drang or the period of storm and stress.

NATURAL PARENTS ... THE SAME PROBLEM

So, suppose you are a set of natural parents reading this. You too may suffer from authority conflict. You too have "Good-guy/bad-guy-itis." Your problem may be a variation on the stepparent scenario. It stems from the mind sets we all bring to parenting. Parents are generally a unique blend of the following patterns:

✔ They try to compensate for the control or lack of control which they experienced as children.

✔ They live with the false belief that letting children have what they want all or most of the time is an act of love.

✔ They try to compensate for the other parent whom they see as being too harsh, thereby sending the child a message that they love the child more, and that he or she may therefore escape from the demands of the other parent.

✔ They are trying to compensate for the other parent whom they see as being too lenient, thereby sending the child a message that they love the child more because they set limits so that the world will not beat the child up when he or she enters it.

Such parents are incapable of parenting effectively and are discounting how damaging their tug of war is, in that it cancels out the child's responsibility for his or her own behavior. BE WRONG IF YOU HAVE TO, BUT BE TOGETHER

All of these patterns may be part of a normal family network. If we can see them as normal outgrowths of a family's attempt to act as a family, we can be more forgiving and tolerant when we encounter them in action. These common behavior patterns in families are rarely talked about. We act as if they do not, or should not exist. This is the root of our lie. We must accept families who fall into these patterns as Nornal Loving, Dysfunctional families, trying to do the best job they can.

The reality is that we just don't sense intuitively how to do the right job; we have to teach one another. Parents from parents, parents from counselors, parents from children, we must learn from one another. The stick behind the shed routine will only get us in trouble. What is to replace it? Should we give up on limits? Decidedly, NO.

JB's Rule #9: When in doubt, Join the Bad Guy

There are few things more tragic than seeing children who are the product of families in which they have been allowed to get away with anything and everything. To become worthwhile human beings, kids must learn that they cannot have everything they want. They also need to have adults say No to them on certain issues. They will never experience this if no one is willing to take the role of the bad guy. Remember, the bad guy probably also loves the kid and views giving the kid limits by saying "no" as an act of love. A kid is even better served when the adults in his life stand side-by-side and say No in stereo when they are dealing with a serious situation. This makes the kid feel secure, knowing there are two people in accord looking after his or her welfare.

My teenage kids knew a family with a son who threw tantrums every time he wanted something. Whenever his parents refused his extravagant demands, he would leave home and camp out in his tree house. Upon his return, his demands would be granted. Stereos, cars, money, ski trips: No matter what the cost, it would be covered by his cowed parents who could not bear to see the boy unhappy. Neither parent was willing to be the bad guy, and the result was a miserable child who was self-centered, selfish, and spoiled. Militant Parents would change the situation around by risking the disapproval of their much-loved child. To say No to a spoiled kid is not saying you don't love him or her. To allow a child to remain spoiled and obnoxious is to turn the child out in the world certain to receive the disapproval of others.

In life, as the Rolling Stones remind us, You Can't always Get What You Want. We often get what we need, however. Regardless of our ages, if it is happiness, we can have it. If it is unhappiness, we can have it. We choose our attitudes toward life. God wants us all to be happy. Usually, we are the ones getting in our own way. It's the same for our kids. They must learn to be happy, even when they are not getting all they want. The term neurotic was once defined as the space that is filled between where I am and where I am going. Most of us are neurotic, but we need not be miserable.

Longing shortens our lives and make us dissatisfied with what we have. When someone tells a kid No, and the kid accepts that there is no manipulating around it by going to the other adult, the kid has a chance to learn limits and boundaries. Granted, the No must be fair and just, but when the good guy and the bad guy consult and reach a decision that is well thought out and in the best interest of the child, they have performed a loving act. Occasionally this may, for the sake of unity, actually have to be a "performance" for one of the parents. Nevertheless, if they appear solid in their decision, the result will be the same.

When I was growing up with my children, I often used the following rather inane drill which they seemed to find amusing. They would ask for something, and I would reply, "No, I am sorry, you can't have that." They would ask again, and I would laughingly respond, "Tell you what, why don't you say, 'I love you Daddy, now can I have it?'" They would then say this and I would respond, "No, I am sorry, but you still can't have it." The purpose of the drill was to reinforce the rule that No meant No. This drill allows the kid to "butter up" the parent, with full knowledge of the game being played by everyone who participates. It was not done to frustrate them or make them angry at me. Instead, the objective was to good-naturedly acknowledge the "butter up" and say No in spite of it!

Healthy, normal American kids should perfect the skill of trying to coerce an authority figure into giving them what they want. This is how they ask to have their needs met. However, parents must also reinforce the idea that they will say No whenever that word is the most appropriate response to a request. Let me reiterate: Saying No to our children for their best good is an act of love. Joining the bad guy much of the time is an act of love and shows support for your partner as well.

JB's RULE #10: NEVER LIE TO YOUR CHILDREN

It is not just children who have problems with lies. Unfortunately, they have no corner on the falsehood market. Sometimes we threaten and don't mean it. We tell them No and later change our answer to Yes when we succumb to pressure and guilt. We Lie Also. There is a damaging hypocrisy that we sometimes allow to develop when our children are really acting out. We escalate our threats and proclamations of serious consequences, but fail to follow through on our menacing words. It would be far better to say nothing at all than to say no or make threats we are not willing to back up with actions. If you mean it say it. If you're not sure, don't threaten when you don't mean it!

Consider the classic teenage example. I have watched this scenario for years. Little Miss Attitude demands to go to the concert "all the other kids" are going to. Actually all the other kids are not going. Only her friend Little Miss Altitude (who is also experimenting with getting high) is trying to go and expects your daughter to join her. Miss Altitude is also using the same line on her parents. Your daughter is told No repeatedly, throws the "mother of all tantrums," locks herself in her room, threatens to kill herself, then climbs out the window at night and attends the concert with the money she has taken from your purse or wallet. And you say, " What's the use? I can't control her." The lie here is that the parent said no, the girl did it anyway, and the parent gave up proclaiming she couldn't control her.

I worked with a tormented mother and father whose son was a heroin addict. He crashed cars, lost jobs, got sent to jail, and stole from the family. For years they threatened him with dire consequences with which they never followed through. I advised repeatedly, "Stop lying to the boy! If you say you are going to kick him out of the home, do it, and stop threatening him. You are lying to him." The sorrow in the father's face was painful to see. Here was a man who deeply regretted the morally and physically deteriorated state his son had reached, but was himself not willing to be truthful. The son was incapable at that time of being honest with his parents. This is part of the disease of addiction. It is not just a family disease, it is family of diseases.

This family was reunited partially because the mother and father changed their position and began to consistently tell the boy the truth. They followed through with what they said, saying No and meaning No. The son is now sober. The father means what he says and says what he means, and, happily, I worked myself out of another job.

No must always mean No But how do you make it stick? I often offer platitudes which suggest goals but don't tell you how to implement them to win. The truth is you can't always win. Sometimes kids are so head-strong that there is nothing you can do to stop them. The trick is to know which battles to fight and which battles to pass on. This is the real dilemma of parenting. We must be careful about selecting our battles.

JB's Rule # 11: Say yes when ever you can!

Yup, that's what I said. Say yes whenever you can. A child who meets with affirmation and encouragement learns to explore and experiment, usually with positive behaviors, when given the freedom to do so. When we can indicate that we trust our children and have confidence in their ability to move forward in appropriate ways, we reinforce their self-esteem and reward them for communicating their desires to us.

Consider young Jason who yearns to play the clarinet. If it is possible, let him have a go at it. If he gives it up later and wants to try another instrument, find a way to let him invest in his change of mind. This time he gets to pay some of the freight charges. But you are telling him yes, letting him experience some accountability while permitting him to change his mind. You are also telling him it is all right to have dreams.

There are age-appropriate and "kid-specific" approaches to this challenge, of course. All children are not created equal. Some can handle more freedom and at earlier ages than others. It is not appropriate to allow some kids to venture into certain behaviors before they are mature enough to handle the consequences of these behaviors (i.e. dating at a very young age).

Part of the paradoxical position kids place parents in is that they push for independence and then resent us if they are not fully protected from the consequences of their actions.

The definition of young may be 13 or 14 for some kids, 15 or 16 for others. It is your call as parents to make this decision. Someone will disagree with you no matter what you do. Remember, the goal is to be a Militant Parent, willing to set limits that work for you, but with which others may not agree.

JB's RULE # 12: FIGHT THE BATTLES
YOU CAN WIN.

No duh. (Teenage vernacular depicting the speaker of the truism as a complete idiot). This is an important one. Trying to control behavior with measures on which we can not or will not follow through brings us to the issue of Optional and Mandatory Behaviors

In the work of the late Paul Wood, MD, we find these helpful models: An Optional behavior is one which we would rather our children would follow, but one which we are not willing to go to any extreme to see that they do. A Mandatory behavior is one which we are willing to go to any length to see followed.

Let me give you some examples and suggest what I believe works. It is important to note that It is up to each parent or parents to decide the battles they will fight for themselves I am only offering options. Remember, a Militant Parent is willing to parent without the approval of others. That includes me. What you choose to do might not be something I would do with my children, but you must follow your own heart. It helps if you also pick battles you can win.

Kenny Rogers sang the words which follow in the song
"The Gambler,"
You gotta know when to hold 'em
Know when to fold 'em
Know when to walk away,
And know when to run.

Chapter Five may help you to decide which battles to pick.

CHAPTER FIVE

PICKING YOUR BATTLES

The best way to prepare for battle is to find out what has worked for other people. You can learn from their mistakes and victories which battles you want to fight. The way we fight our battles is far more important than what we fight about, but more about that later...

Now the issue is to pick and choose. Ask other people how and why they have declared their battles. Make a list of the issues and go over them one by one: the room, the car, mating in the house, money. If it worked for them, find out how. If not, find out why.

Much of the problem we face when we consider undertaking such battles is that we may be zeroing in on a behavior and trying to make it Mandatory, when we should be considering it Optional. There are a number of things to be evaluated: How old is your child? Is there support from your partner? Do you need a coach? Has the kid or spouse involved become the parent you never confronted or revolted against? Don't intellectualize all this too much It will give you a headache. But don't disregard it, either. If the shoe fits, you may need to wear it.

As we wind our way through the maze of problem-atic issues, I will offer some insight as to how to address them rationally. This is my version of how you might deal with problems. There is someone else who tried something different. This is not a manual on how to do it. It is a book about possibilities. No one has written the definitive parenting manual. If they had, it would not work on your kids anyway.

POSSIBLE BATTLE #1: THEIR ROOM

The single most common complaint I hear from parents is about the kid's room. This represents a working model for the problem. First... ask yourself, or yourselves, if this is an Optional or Mandatory, problem category. If you are willing to go to any lengths to see the room is clean, then put on your armor, "lock and load," and prepare for battle. Consider the following steps:

1. Tell the kid to clean her room and keep it clean. This order will not damage her delicate psyche. It will prepare her for a world that works better with order rather than chaos.

2. Tell the kid you are serious, but do not threaten consequences. As a matter of fact, explain that you are not going to let her know what the consequences are. This is in keeping with the way the real world works. We don't always know exactly what will happen when we test authority. Keep her guessing about what you will do. [That way, if you're not sure what you will do, you can figure it out later.] After she gets used to the idea that it is dangerous for her to test you on some things, you will have more compliance with less strain.

3. If the kid does not respond (and some kids probably will not since they remember exactly what your past track record has been on such issues far better than you do), go down to the hardware store and purchase an outside lock of the same brand you have in your home. (Examples included Kwikset, Schlage, and Weiser.) Do not buy a 'privacy lock', the type that can be opened with one of those odd looking little keys that everyone loses. The problem

here is that a paper clip will work just as well.

4. Place a security lock (with a key like the one that fits the front door) on the door of the room or bathroom. Face the lock to the hallway and take the key. Lock the window to the room or bathroom because she will go through it. Then

✔ Take the key and keep it in a safe place.

✔ Expect one outraged kid.

✔ Do not shame or lecture the kid at this time. It will only make the situation worse.

✔ Be ready for the kid to ask how long this little experiment will last.

✔ Whatever the immediate outcome, don't unlock the room just yet.

However, do explain that this first "blast across the bow" will last for 24 hours, and that after that time you will again ask her to clean up the room or bathroom. Tell her exactly what you demand. Rehearse it or write it down ahead of time. Know your script. Be brief. Say something like, "I want you to make your bed each day, keep the hamster's cage clean, and pick up the big chunks." Just leave it at that and walk away. Don't predict that she will end up like a Charles Manson groupie, tell her she has the devil in her, or admit that you are ashamed of yourself as a parent. None of this matters. What does matter is that you are following through on what you said. So be consistent.

CAUTION: Do not under any circumstances lock the kid IN the room. This would be going too far. It is not safe to lock kids in their rooms; they might not be able to get out in a fire. It is considered "false imprisonment," a term you can probably readily identify with since it is what you feel some of the time <u>with your kids</u>. Never lock any members of your family up - it's a major abusive "bozo no -no."

After you have completed all the above steps, just wait out the time period. She may say, "I can't get my makeup out of the locked bathroom." She may say, "I can't go to school because I can't get to my clothes." Keep your cool. Be calm, and hold to the limit. After the 24-hr period, it is time to open up the room or bathroom.

The final step is to have a brief discussion with the kid reviewing the entire drill. Ask if she knows what you want from her. If she does not, reiterate exactly what you expect, and remember to be brief. Don't dwell on feelings, for it is action that you are after. An employer who wants her work space kept clean does not particularly care how she feels. You are giving her a gift to prepare her for the world.

THE FUNCTION OF TIME:

Time factors are important here. Most things in families resolve themselves within 24 hours. If this does not work, 72 hours is the magical number. Remember these time frames when you experience crisis in the family. We tend to see crises as life and death situations, but they generally pass in a relative short period of time. In the many years I worked as a probation officer, I saw kids act out, the family would be in chaos, and yet the situation would usually be over within 72 hours, no matter what anyone did. It is not necessary to extend punishments for a long time. Nothing good comes of it.

WHAT IF YOU DON'T CARE ABOUT THE MESSY ROOM?

Suppose you and you and the other parent do not care about the room. Great! That problem is solved.

Still another intermediate possibility is that you can place a self-closing device on the door so it will shut automatically. This will prevent others from having to see the mess inside. Of course, to close it in the first place, you may need to kick clothes or dishes (whereon the contents may have turned into a science project) away from the door. So, be brave.

CLOTHES AND DISHES WHICH HAVE TURNED INTO SCIENCE PROJECTS:

Clothes and dishes are another bone of contention. Some moms and dads see themselves as a support system for the guests in their houses... the kids. Bad career move. Kids need to learn to take care of themselves. This means clothes, taking the dishes back to their original home, and picking up the big chunks in the room. If they fail to pick up their clothes, and you are still doing the wash...don't. Let them take over. If they don't, let them run out of clothes. Now it's their problem and not your problem. [I promise you they will come up with some very creative lines to try to make you feel guilty, but in the long run, they will like themselves better if they are not invalids in the laundry room.]

If the kid cannot return the dishes from the kitchen, insist that no dishes leave the kitchen. It is one thing to make a mess of one's own room. It is another to behave irresponsibly with the family's collective property. If the dishes do not migrate back, don't let them migrate out.

With well over 75% of women working in most American families, it is not fair to mom to have to be a support system for all the domestic chores in the house. Children with both types of plumbing systems can learn to take care of the laundry and the dishes. We are well past the misconception that men are born with screwdrivers and hammers in their hands and that women are born holding pots, pans, and Tide containers.

I was so pampered as a teenager (and later as a husband), that at 28 I had the skill to take apart the washer and dryer to repair it, but I could not operate it. Before we reach adulthood, we all need to know how to function so that in emergencies and as part of our responsibilities as supportive helpmates, we can do the wash, perform at least survival cooking, and manage the cleaning. It is also handy for both sexes to know how to start the lawnmower and change a tire.

I worked with a mom one time who took all the stuff her kids left lying around in the house and placed it in a "trash-can jail" in the garage. It stayed there for one month, and was then released to be returned to its owner, after the owner washed it.

If you don't address the issue of dirty clothes, many kids' rooms will smell like Phys-Ed. So take a stand somewhere. The order of options are, from lower to higher...

✔ Ignore the whole thing and concentrate on other battles.

✔ Have them close the door, then ignore what is inside.

✔ Place a self-closing device on the door.

✔ Do not do the laundry if it does not get to where it should be in the laundry room.

Tell them to clean the room or bathroom.

✔ Place a 24-hour or 72-hour lock on the room or bathroom, with no lecture or false battle threats. Hold to the banishment till they get the picture, and, finally release the room from bondage.

POSSIBLE BATTLE #2: YOUR MONEY AND YOUR STUFF

As adults we experience intense feelings of personal violation when our children get into our stuff. They must learn not to do so if they are to get along in the world. The journey toward respecting the property of other family members can be a difficult one.

YOUR MONEY

If you have ghosts taking your money, lock your money up. This may sound a little negative, but to some kids, available cash is like a Maserati sitting in the drive with the keys in it. Get a safe; get a lock box; get a lock on your own room. If you don't want them to take it and they have a poor track record, stop sniveling and do something about it.

CLOTHES

If you are tired of your dresses and sweaters being worn by your teenagers, lock up your closet. This is one of the most volatile issues involved in parenting teenagers, the personal violation which results from having items of apparel taken from our wardrobe. It isn't just mom's stuff, either. I remember being outraged at seeing my daughter wearing my favorite T-shirt, which she claimed was justified because she got it out of the dryer.

Clothing for teenage girls follows a migratory pattern, mostly in any direction away from your home. If they have lost track of something because it has been loaned, don't buy a new one. If they have lost something of yours, insist that they buy you a new one, lock your door again, and get on with life. Twenty years from now you won't remember which belt was missing. Take heart that this will all pass.

The same is true of tools. My kids think I have a screwdriver fetish. They think I should go to Screwdrivers Anonymous, and my wife to Screwanon. Well, I got tired of having all my screwdrivers float out of their drawer, so every time I noticed screwdrivers on sale, I stocked up. Now that the kids have moved out, I am the proud owner of a drawer completely filled with screwdrivers. It solved the problem then, and it provides something for the family to continue to laugh about.

POSSIBLE BATTLE #3: THE TELEPHONE

If you read the table of contents, you probably flipped to this section first, just to see how it was handled. If you have a teenager and a telephone in the same house, you have a problem. But you already know that. The kid is out of control on your phone, and you have to pick up the freight. Get a phone for her. Let her pay the bill. Thus you accomplish several things.

One, the calls will be more personalized and so will the bill. Two, your phone will not be ringing at 12 o'clock midnight. Of course, it's not always the fault of the kid when someone calls too late or too early for your schedule.

It is, however, very annoying, especially when they hang up so as not to be confronted by you. Believe me, it is worth the peace of mind to let all the kids share one phone: the one that is not yours. They don't need to have all the features like call waiting and all the other bells and gadgets. If they simply can't live without these features, let them pay for them - with their money that they earn.

POSSIBLE BATTLE #4: SMOKING

The previous example is probably not as important as this one to the overall quality of the life of your child. However, it is a classic example of the difference in picking battles we can or cannot win. Remember the rule: Do not take on a battle you cannot win.

To win the smoking battle, you must follow the kid around 24 hours a day to enforce compliance. Are you willing to do that?

SMOKING IN YOUR HOME

A battle you can win is to insist that kids not smoke in your house. This symbolizes respect, which we all must learn. If you find the kid smoking in his or her room, ask them to leave it (temporarily). Restrict them from the room until they agree to not smoke in it again. Smoking in the outside world is potentially a very serious danger in restricted areas (e.g. an airplane restroom). Why should it be allowed in your home if you do not wish it?

Another consideration here is whether or not you smoke. If you do, stop! Let all the family know how hard it is. Ask them to support you, and ask them to understand how hard it is to quit. In my many decades of working with alcoholics, street drug addicts, and heroin addicts, I have consistently heard it said that it is more difficult to quit cigarettes than any other kind of recreational chemical.

Or, offer an incentive plan to each kid. If you are a non-smoker on your 18th burthday, you win $250.00. This is a lot better than nagging them to stop when they have no intention to do so.

POSSIBLE BATTLE #5: PICKING FRIENDS

This is clearly a battle within the Optional behavior area. You probably can't win if you make it a Mandatory because you can't follow kids around. What you can make Mandatory is that they not allow someone in your home you don't approve of. Remember, it's your home. This battle is, of course, age specific. If we are talking about an 8-year old versus a 14-year old, the control is much more effective for the 8-year old. Teenagers are much too mobile to monitor, especially once they have wheels. You may be able to apply restriction for a short period of time, but prolonged restriction from friends is unrealistic.

Kids can go underground with this one and win the battle when you are not looking. A better move is to initiate a dialog about why you think certain friends or acquaintances may not be a good influence on your kid. Past this discussion, if they persist, you have every right to banish or physically evict some kids from your home.

If you need to add humor to the situation you may say things like, "I don't care for the chain hanging from the ring that goes from Duke's nose to the ring in his ear." The kid will then point out she thinks it is cool, and you can say you don't approve because the chain is gold and the rings are stainless steel, making a poor fashion statement.

Whatever you say, remember that you have the right to set the limits on who comes into your home. It is your home, and if someone is particularly offensive to you, you can ask your child not to have this person in while still allowing the child to choose companions while he or she is away from your home (which the child will probably do whether you allow it or not). It is important to frame the issue this way because it respects the kid's prerogative while requiring your wishes to be respected as well.

POSSIBLE BATTLE #6: MOVING INTO PARTY TIME OR THE "ARMED GUARD PHASE" (OR "THE THREE BEARS")

A common battle many parents of teenagers fight relates to the issue of what goes on at home when the parents are away for a day or longer. Absent parents often return from even short outings to find there has been a party at their home.

Most kids are not rotten to the core. They sometimes just have a few friends over, but one friend they tell tells another friend, and that friend tells another friend, and before long there is a wild party going on. Parents are then left footing the bill for the damage and liability. Throwing a large party which gets out of control is usually not the intention of the kid. It occurs because other teenagers are inextricably drawn to a home which is without adult supervision.

Remember the fairy tale of the three bears? Someone had been eating their porridge, and someone had been sleeping in their beds? You may know Mama and Papa bears' feelings after discovering the signs of someone mating in your bed, depleting your liquor cabinet, or leaving cigarette burns on what is left of your carpet. At this point, you know the feeling of personal violation.

You have several alternatives when this situation occurs. You may take the kids with you next time (possibly a fate worse than death). Or you may tell them they must stay someplace other than home. Make sure you lock the house, however, and make sure you have all the keys or this option will not work. Make sure all the windows are locked also, because kids are masters at breaking into their own homes.

Another alternative is to consider the Armed Guard Phase of parenting teenagers. In this move, you hire an adult who has only two directives in his or her job description. One is to call for reinforce-ments (police) if anyone is in the house who does not belong. The second is to comport himself or herself so that the kids tell you that they don't particularly like the person or his or her attitude when you return from your trip. This person may come and go from the house while you are gone. But the kids should not know when this house guard plans to come back, so they are constantly kept on good behavior. What is first and foremost is the requirement that the kids know the house guard will take action if unauthorized troops enter the militarized zone which was previ-ously your home.

This scenario sounds a little humorous, but It Is Very Serious. As a matter of fact, it may be a matter of life and death. It is not uncommon to hear of kids who die prior to the age of 21 as a result of drunk driving after unsupervised parties. Sadly, it is not uncommon for the host of the party to be a minor, with parents not in attendance or parents who allowed drinking to go on in the home. Serious injury to property, people (shootings occur at teenage parties even in stable neighborhoods), and open drug use are all possible consequences of such unsupervised situations.

Let me stress the alcohol issue. Drinking alcohol continues to be the number one drug problem in the country. For some reason, drug and alcohol specialists like myself have been unsuccessful in conveying this disaster strongly enough. Alcohol causes more car crashes, violence, and impulsive criminal behavior than all other drugs combined! "Thank God, they are just drinking," is not an acceptable statement referring to teenagers. If you haven't noticed, it is no longer all right for adults either. Society is getting much harsher on drunk drivers due to the damage and wreckage of lives they leave behind. Don't leave alcohol in your house unlocked when you are away. They will try it, just as you and I did.

Let me also say a word about supervised parties. Many adults think it is cool to allow their teenagers and young adults to throw a party that is supervised. There is no way you, or any number of adults, can control a large party where lots of alcohol is being consumed. The consequences are exactly the same as at an unsupervised party — fights, aggressive behavior, and drunk driving—and this is without the party being crashed by a local gang or unwanted guests from a rival high school.

We are making a little headway in the drinking-and-driving problem with designated driver programs, education about alcohol and drugs, and programs like D.A.R.E. But these are not enough, nor will they ever be enough. We are a drinking society. We must set an example as parents and refuse to tolerate drinking and driving in ourselves or in our kids. I know this stance may turn a few of you off, but I would rather risk a little anger than see one more young life sacrificed to a drunk kid behind the wheel.

POSSIBLE BATTLE #7:   MONEY AND JOBS

Kids want "stuff" just as we adults do. The problem is, we are the ones who are seen as the source of the money and the "stuff." Since we want to show our children we love them, we often do it with material things. Many people as adults face shopping extrava-gantly as a continuing problem. When they feel depressed or unloved, they buy more "stuff."

We often think kids need allowances so that they can learn to handle money. This, unfortunately, does not generally work because they learn to manage our money and often not very well. A better alternative is to give each child a job. If he does the job, he gets paid. If he does not do the job, another kid gets the job. If a member of the immediate family does not want the job and the money, hire a kid down the street.

I cannot stress enough how important it is not to lecture kids on this one. Don't shame them or call their actions wrong; just don't pay them. They will figure it out.

An "allowance" places kids on welfare. They begin to assume they have the right to receive the money for no effort. If you expect them to do a job to get the money, don't call it an allowance! Call it a salary or payment for services rendered.

None of us who are able-bodied have an inalien-able right to receive money for no effort. So structure the finances to reflect reality. Borrowing money is a real part of the financial world. The world of the family should be structured the same. A person who shows integrity with money is allowed to borrow more money. A person builds up a credit record, and this dictates his or her ability to eventually buy large items like cars and homes.

Kids are in the borrowing business. However, we do not always act like a real bank. We loan, they borrow. They do not pay back on time (or at all), and we do nothing about it.

A common scenario is the teenager or young adult who wants a new car. We place the loan on our credit, the kid does not pay it back on time (or at all), and we make the payment. A better reaction is to take the car back just like the bank would. Don't tell the kid he or she is not Ok. Just take it back! Sure, this causes problems. She has a hang nail and cannot get to work. He breaks up with his girlfriend and becomes depressed. However, none of these tragedies are the concern of the real bank. Banks could care less what happens to us personally. A TRW report does not have a column that says, "This person had a difficult childhood and should be treated with special consid-eration." The bank just wants the money or the car back. We need to think and act on the same terms to help them to be ready for the real world.

CARS:

It doesn't matter whether it is your car or theirs. The car scene can still cost you. Cars in America are, to an extent, a rite of passage for male and female teenagers. There was a time when it was only the male, but now both sexes see a set of wheels as a God-given right. It is not. In fact, with the mortality rate as high as it is for teenagers, the dangers of, as well as the liability for, teenage driving presents a serious problem. Let me give you some grim examples.

A family has a daughter who suffers a serious head injury while drunk at a party. While taking anti-seizure medication (resulting from the head injury) and still drinking, she continues to use the family car and crashes head on into an oncoming car, killing her passenger and severely injuring all the passengers in the other car. With court pending, and a guaranteed jail term (set forth by the California legislature in all drunk driving convictions), her parents borrow on their house and pay an attorney $35,000 to protect the girl from the consequences which she is going to suffer whether she has an attorney or not.

My advice to such a family is to avoid the private lawyer and allow the kid to get a public defender. Otherwise, the kids in the family who have good jobs, are going to college, and have done nothing wrong could end up being denied family resources because the parents are taking care of the kid who has behaved irresponsibly.

Consider another example of a family which did not transfer a car to their kid's name when she turned 18. The daughter got drunk, crashed the car, and the family was sued because it was still in their name. The consequence? They lost their house, their own new car, and again, the money which should have gone to helping the other kids in the home who were doing well.

So what are the options if you have decided to let your teenagers and young adults drive?

My wife and I provided each of our four kids with a car. Beyond that point they were on their own. That is, they had to pay the insurance. So if they got tickets or caused accidents, they could feel the pinch. They had to pay for gas, so if they drove their friends all over town, they had to meet the expense. They also had to pay for tires and repairs.

One of the worst case scenarios is for the kid to pay nothing, have complete access to a car she hasn't paid for, drive it with gas she has not bought, leave it to be repaired with money she did not provide, and crash it to have your insurance increase, only to be paid for with money she has not earned.

The interesting thing in this example is that therapists like myself see people every day who do not appreciate their parents for doing this type of enabling. To the contrary, they are furious at the parents for not allowing them to grow up.

Here is still another suggestion to consider: Under no circumstances should a kid be allowed to drink and drive or use drugs and drive. If you don't think you can do anything about it, think again. You can, and you must. If not for the safety of your child, then for the safety of all the other persons in the car or in the path of that car.

My wife and I provided our daughter with a new VW convertible on her 16th birthday, which she drove while under the influence of alcohol. We took the car away from her as promised. But some months later, while the car was parked across the street, she sat out in the parked car and got drunk with a friend. We then towed the car away and placed it in storage until she was 18. Our feeling was that the car had been given to her. Her permission to drive it, however, was at our option.

The option aspect of the driver's license is not known to all parents. They grant their child permission to drive, but can withdraw that permission by filling out a form with the Department of Motor Vehicles. It is not a right to drive a car. It is a privilege. Again, you have the option to grant that permission to the child, and you have the right to withdraw that permission. Your teenage children need to have this information.

POSSIBLE BATTLE #8: GRADES IN SCHOOL

"But they are not living up to their potential." Yeah, I know, but are you? I'm not, but the big difference between myself and others is that I have come to realize and accepted that no one does. Most kids are pedaling as fast as they can. That is the most we can expect of them. The important thing is that kids are up to skill level in the main subject areas. Remember, the report card evaluates the kid's performance, not yours. It is far better to get a tutor (possibly some high school kid recommended by a church) than to take it out on the kid's hide. Kids need to know that they are responsible for their academic success. You can explain to them the importance of grades to their further education, but do not nag. Many persons in history [like Ben Franklin who flunked the 10th grade twice] did not do well initially, but gained momentum later in life.

THE GRADE GAME FOUGHT IN VAIN:

I have seen family after family fight the grade game in vain. Parents battle night after night to get the kid to do his homework. The kid finally does it, but then does not take it to school.

You can take on this battle if you want, but it may not be worth it. Getting a certain grade in a class is not going to make the difference in the kid's life forever. Even a kid with dismal grades in high school can still go to community college and on from there if he wants to later. What is important to each student is to achieve the academic skills needed to read, write, and do mathematics. Because a student does not excel in high school does not always mean he or she will not succeed in life.

POSSIBLE BATTLE # 9: RUNNING AWAY FROM HOME

Kids are supposed to leave home. For centuries, they have not always left under the best of circumstances. Running away often occurs following a major blow up. Usually, it is the full moon (No, I'm not kidding), and the problem will pass, along with the onset of the new moon, which gets us back to the 72-hour crisis pattern I talked about in Chapter Five. Anyway, the runaway incident usually passes with little or no intervention, so do not make it any worse than it is.

When runaway behavior is building, there is often a great deal of tension in the house. It is important to not let this tension escalate to physical confrontation. The rule is: WHEN PHYSICAL CONFRONTATIN IS NEEDED TO CONTROL A KID, SHOW THE KID THE DOOR! If you try to stop the kid from leaving, and a physical confrontation ensues which leaves marks on or causes serious injuries to the child, you can be locked up or at least expect a visit from Child Protective Services. Don't lose your composure! You and the kid may not even remember why he or she wanted to leave ten years from now. However, you will both probably always remember who got physically hurt and how. The children who watched or heard will remember also. Family violence memories do not go away. Kids are supposed to go away... happily... at least someday.

You can try this little maneuver on the kid who has taken off for parts unknown. When the kid calls (and a kid usually does call after a couple of days), tell him you are not sure if you are going to let him come home and ask him to call you back in a day or so. Sound unkind? Well, maybe. But there is a worse case scenario than this one. If you let the kid have what he

wanted before he ran away, he will be running away
every time he wants something.

What you are achieving in this runaway situation
is a "power-reverse." It is somewhat like the boy and
girl game of "The boy chases the girl until she catches
him." Or "Now I've got you exactly where you want
me." What you are doing is saying, "You can't quit me,
you're fired," claiming the responsibility for what
happens next as the parent and head of the house.

One additional note is needed about running away.
When a kid has run away, you should call the police.
In most states, they will not arrest a runaway, but will
facilitate the kid's return. A kid may need to be taken
into protective custody for a short time, but this is a
positive alternative to having him run on the streets.
Giving the police a report allows the child to be
placed on a missing persons list so that he can be
identified in case of an accident.

The open streets of many large cities in the United
States are not safe places for a kid. Let us hope your
kid does not end up there. Generally, a child will
return home in a short time. Sadly, the kids who do
end up living on the streets are often kids rejected or
abused by their families, or who are not willing to
accept any limits from their parents regarding their
use of alcohol and drugs and or their sexual behavior.

WHEN THINGS GET PHYICAL:

The only physical restraint needed when a child
becomes physically abusive is to hold the kid down.
Do not hit, threaten with Juvenile Hall, or propose
anything else you cannot follow through with. Just
restrain kids who are a danger to themselves or
others. If you can't restrain them, get out of their way.
Leave until the tension passes. Better to walk away

than to be physically violent and regret it for the rest of your life. If necessary, call the police. They are trained to handle such matters, and they usually will not hurt a kid unless it is absolutely unavoidable.

A technique recommended by Tough Love is to lock the kid out if she doesn't come home on time or has run away. This is a variation on the "power reverse" above. You tell the kid she can't come in, but give her an address of a place she can stay, preferably with someone whom she doesn't like. This places the responsibility back on the child. You are not required by law to place your roof over kids' heads; you are required to place a roof over their heads.

WHEN SIBLINGS BECOME PHYSICALLY VIOLENT:

If you listen in on the sibling fighting of many children, you will hear a variety of squeals, howls, accusations, and crying. To listen in on some of this fighting, one would think limbs are being torn off and eyes plucked out. Drama is often at the heart of this ongoing sibling conflict, and the audience is the parent or adult who is being sucked into a bottomless pit of adjudicating the winner.

What is fascinating about this drama is the ability of the underdog to continually come out the victor at the end of the power struggle. The victory comes when the parent intervenes on behalf of the poor, helpless, usually younger, weaker child. Parental intervention generally clenches the victory for the underdog.

Many siblings fight. It is normal. It is also extremely nerve wracking to hear the bickering, screaming, and squealing. Rather than intervening in sibling quarreling with a judgment call that deter-mines winners and losers (usually the underdog), the wise parent stays out of the fight unless certain boundaries are crossed. These may include but are not restricted to:

✔ When blood is drawn.
✔ When bones are broken.
✔ When the house is damaged as a result of the fighting.
✔ When the yelling, screaming, and squealing threatens parental sanity.

In all other instances, it is probably more judicious to mind your own business. They will work it out. If they don't, and you can't stand the fighting, place them in separate corners until they are willing to get along (with no comment as to who Was specifically at fault), then allow them to return to the arena when they are ready to behave. When the sparring starts up again (and it will), separate them again and repeat the same drill. If you take a stand in favor of one kid, the problem will become more difficult to solve and may go on for a lifetime. Younger brothers and sisters are masterful at sucking in adults to referee the fights they start and expect parents to finish, proclaiming them the victors.

INFORMAL FOSTER HOMES:

When hostilities continue out of hand or become physical, it is possible to let the kid move in with a surrogate family. To avoid formal foster care, many families work this sort of arrangement out among themselves informally. The parent may wish to pay the surrogate family for helping out with the kid. Or, the kid can get a job and pay her own way.

POSSIBLE BATTLE # 10: BRINGING OTHER PUPPIES HOME

Kids love to bring home stray puppies without your invitation and sanction. This may cause you work, expense and frustration. Generally, the kid acquires the pets, then leaves them with you to take care of because the dorm, apartment or jail he is moving to will not accept pets.

This unauthorized extension of your hospitality can also be a problem when the puppy is of the human kind, some poor lost soul who has no place to go because he or she is from a home run by the "parent from hell." If you take the kid in, in time you may also be assuming the role of the "parent from hell" and come to know why the other parent or parents acted as they did.

There is a great, engaging illusion perpetuated by children who have left homes to live in alternate homes. The illusion is that the parents of this poor stray are hard-hearted, blood-sucking, horn-headed monsters who eat their young. They are actually, of course, just like you and me, and they have problems with their kids just like we do.

A miraculous thing happens to families who take our kids in. Within a month of the time they do so, a friend or relative happens to come in from out of town and they no longer have room for the kid in their house. I have heard this excuse so many times, I almost laugh when it resurfaces.

Another phenomenon occurs early on when someone takes a kid in. The rescuing family comments to us (if we are speaking) that our kid is so wonderful that they would like ten more just like her. Stay mellow. The same thing would happen if their kid had moved into our home.

The fact is, we have not done such a bad job of socializing the kid. She knows how to behave in public when she wants to, and she knows how to behave in someone else's home. Surprise, surprise the toilet training drills did work, and we have not raised the "monster from hell" we previously thought we had.

What eventually happens in the new home is that the kid's old behaviors begin to emerge, including not picking up after herself and eating the equivalent of her weight every day. Soon, the rescuing parent is feeling used and abused by the situation, and the kid is returned home to start another round of attempted emancipation.

Understsnading The Victim Triangle

There is a triangle that forms in many social relationships. It consists of The Rescuer, The Victim and The Perpetrator. Police are very familiar with this dance:

> They are called out on a domestic violence (an oxymoron) problem between husband and wife. The police walk in, see the wife being physically abused, and begin to arrest the husband. He resists and she (the wife) comes to the rescue of the husband.

The wife started as the Victim and is now the Rescuer, the husband started as the Perpetrator, and is now the Victim. The police started as the Rescuers, and are now the Perpetrators.

A Word to Rescuers

Kids are regular champions at being Professional Victims. They can suck any of us in with their ruminations about how awful their parents are. Some parents are awful. And so are some kids. It takes time to discover the truth, so keep in mind that you too can get drawn into this drama. Take time to talk to the parents of any child you take in. You will need them eventually. The better the relationship you have established, the more you can sort through the problem.

The easiest person to "hook" within this victim scenario is the ex-spouse, when one exists. Guilt greatly distorts some of our perceptions. When little Johnny is living with Dad and his new girlfriend (the "hussy"), it is easy to misperceive all negative behavior as originating with the devil herself reincarnated. After all, isn't she a home-wrecker? Kids play this card to the hilt and become very skilled at manipulating the insecurities and jealousies of the estranged parents.

What I suggest here is a alignment between as many persons in this situation as possible. If mom will not talk in the same room with stepmom (or girlfriend) work on alignment between father and stepmom (girlfriend), alone. Better to have at least two people aligned on behalf of the kid than having all parties working against one another. If dad does not honor the opinions and suggestions of the new parent in the family, there will be hell to pay. Often a "friend" or step-parent can accurately see the manipulation and games of the kid. Father, however, in this scenario, does not see the new parent figure coming from love and therefore tries to compensate the kid for all the previous distress which has been brought on the kids by the break up of up the original family unit.

HERE ARE SOME SUMMARY SUGGESTIONS:

✔Bring all parent and surrogate parents together if possible.

✔If the other parent team will not participate, draft as many persons onto the team as possible.

✔You can help by keeping your home a place where they experience consistency and follow through. Kids do not get consistent disciplinary structure when they go from one life experience to another (e.g. school classes, work, different shifts at the same job, etc.).

✔Remember that it is normal for kids to play off authority figures to get the best deal they can. It came with their programming when they were born! If possible check out what the "other side" has offered the kid before getting drawn into a bidding war for privileges or possessions.

✔Keep in mind that the parent figures, some in-laws, and counselors can see that guilt is being used as a tool of manipulation. The natural parent (who may be blind to it) needs to recognize their perception. Be open to the insights of objective third parties if possible.

✔Remember that teenagers and some young adults do not get along with adults anyway, so the problem may lie with the kid and not always the adult. Don't take the blame for something that is not your fault.

CHAPTER SIX

CHAPTER SIX

WHEN THE GEESE MIGRATE HOME

Geese, ducks, swallows, homing pigeons, and kids migrate home. It is not in the genes of the kids, however; it is part of a complex change in our social structure. The "X-Generation" has a new set of problems which no other generation has faced. They were told that if they went to college, they would have the world by the tail. That's the problem. They have the world by the wrong end. It's one more reason to think they are victims. We feel so sorry for them and contribute to their failure to emancipate themselves by continuing to take care of them. We must, in small increments such as having them take over their car payments, insurance, food expenses, debt, and lodging, let them grow up and assume responsibility for their own lives.

As parents we contribute to the problem of children who refuse to live independently by allowing them to continue the process of growing-up well into their twenties, thirties, and sometimes upward. We get hooked by a number of factors which we cannot seem to discount. This chapter will help you to look at some of these factors and make a stand, if you need to.

NOTE: OVER-RESPONSABLE PARENTS PRODUCE UNDER RESPONSABLE CHILDREN

Think about it. Up to now we have been saying the same thing in different ways:

Don't do for them what they can do for themselves.

Work yourself out of a job.

Create an independent child.

If they don't need you to survive in the world, they will like you and themselves better, and they will participate in the family because they want to, not because they have to.

Kids who have passed into adulthood and who migrate home are like SLUGS. They sleep all day, stay up all night, and leave slime wherever they go. They will eat your Creeping Charlie plant... and then blame you for not providing additional provisions. Let's take a look at some common scenarios.

SCENARIO #1: KID GOES TO COLLAGE, FLUNKS OUT (OR ISN'T GOING WHEN HE SAYS HE IS), AND RETURNS TO LIVE AT HOME

We all want to help our kids. The trick is to figure out what is helpful and what is harmful. Much of the time we are doing something harmful when we think we are helping. Even when what we do is harmful, it is usually done out of love. That is important. Seeing the motive of the other people in our lives as kind and loving has a bearing on how we approach them and how they approach us. Recognizing a positive motive helps us to be less critical of the causes of their actions. Each of us needs to understand that what we are doing and what the other parent is doing is being done out of love, even if it doesn't work.

If your kid is not producing in life, Take Her Off Welfare... If she goes to school and does not like it... Oh, well. That's not your business. Often a kid is college bound, but is not motivated to achieve because she has not worked in the real world and learned what she can or cannot do without a skill, vocation, or profession. Letting her work, travel (at her expense), or move out are all parts of letting her learn about motivation.

If a semester goes by and a kid is not producing in school, ask to see his grades. If you discover he is not accumulating units, change the rules of support. Tell him to pay for school himself or to get a student loan. If he completes the semester, you will reimburse him. What happens in many families is that the kids are not working hard on achieving goals because they are not their goals, they are your goals. They are being asked to fulfill goals you have had for yourself or for them, and they know they are living out a lie. If you think college or new skill training is a good idea, go yourself, and stop trying to tell them what they should do with their lives.

Over my many years as a therapist, I have worked with numerous kids who were not sure what they wanted to do when they grew up... so, they didn't grow up. There must be a shift in the consciousness of a kid toward having his own dreams and goals. Dreams which are the parents' may carry him for a while, but later, if they do not become the kid's dreams, his life will not be complete or satisfying.

When kids return home from college or are living on their own, they act as if they are heroes returning from the war. What, no party for them? No banner? No band? They are often outraged that you would expect them to lift a hand in the home. That they could help with dishes, laundry, shopping for food, and carrying in the groceries that you bought is beyond their comprehension, and a major imposition if they are watching TV, talking on the phone, or finishing off the leftovers you were planning to serve for dinner.

It is critical that you and your spouse convey to your children that they are now adults and that they must shoulder adult responsibilities. At the root of many of these coming-of-age problems is a family which is going through a traumatic transition. A kid leaving home leaves a hole in the heart of one or both parents. Usually, however, it is just one parent. The other is quite OK with the absence and the impending solitude.

There is an old saying about families: "The kids left home, the dog died, and we got a divorce." Sad, huh? The passage of kids to the next stage of their lives marks the passage of parents to the next stage of their lives as well. This is painful sometimes and forces us to look at our purpose in life. What is our purpose? I think it is to serve others, create, love, and laugh. The rest is just an exercise of daily routine. Are we still being creative? Are we pursuing our dreams? Are there goose bumps in our lives on a regular basis?

EMOTIONAL INCEST:

When a kid leaves home, the parents must look at their relationship (or lack of relationship). The showdown often comes between the parents when one says, "If you don't let him come home, I am leaving." (One might do well to take the threatening spouse up on this offer). When a kid comes between two parents, there is a powerful shift and a valuable lesson to be learned. The parent has just symbolically married the kid and agreed to make a child more important than his or her mate. This phenomenon has come to be known as Emotional Incest.

There may be nothing inappropriate going on sexually, but the bond of the parent to the child assuming greater importance than the bond of spouse to spouse can be devastating in some families. The parent may sometimes attempt to turn the child into his or her counselor, therapist, or priest/confessor. Such a parent may seek the constant companionship of the child and expect the child to provide love and emotional security. Too bad for the kids caught in this trap. Too bad for the parent who is relegated to compete with a child for the role of marriage partner while trying to parent the child rival at the same time.

Some of us must choose in our marriages between our spouse and a child. This becomes necessary when a spouse will not or cannot accept our unreasonable deference to a child or children. It is, of course, a sad state of affairs, and it places a great burden on the child, making him or her the fall guy for a failed marriage.

It is cruel for a parent to turn away from his or her children and abandon them in favor of a new partner. When such a decision is made, resentment is felt by the children and former family, and guilt is felt by the abandoning parent. I cannot remember a single relationship working in which the parent is asked to abandon a former family when he or she does not wish to do so.

It is quite possible the children, teenagers, and others will not like the new partner. This is understandable. However, it is unconscionable to ask the parent to never see, talk to, or help the children of the former marriage as they grow. A possible alternative is for the parent to see them without the new partner being present, but this can be difficult. It is, however, far better than abandonment. In time, and when children grow up, families are often reunited, and may grow to even love one another. The kids and new partner do not owe this to one another; relationships are formed over time and struggle. When a child receives constant messages from the abandoned parent about how bad the new surrogate parent is, it is difficult for the child to form an unbiased opinion.

HERE ARE SOME SUMMARY SUGGESTIONS:

✔ Do not compare the love you feel for your children to the love you feel for your spouse or new partner. This love is not and should not be compared.

✔ Don't assume the attitude and behavior of your teenager is due solely to the break up in the family. Some teenagers are surly anyway; eventually, most outgrow it.

✔ Do not allow the children to push the limits and buttons of the new spouse or partner. BACK UO YOUR PARTNER, The kids will survive it.

✔ Do not badmouth your former spouse to the kids, even if you know he or she is badmouthing you. Take out your anger somewhere else. Don't place the kids in an impossible situation where they are asked to turn on the absent parent whom they may still love.

✔ Do tell the kids the other parent loves them, if you know this to be true.

✔ Do tell the kids you love them.

✔ Do support limits set by all members of the parenting team, including the school, if you can. The kids will all do better with such a coalition.

✔ Do remember that the kid will grow up some day and that many wounds do heal in time.

A significant number of relationships break up because of problems over the kids. This is a terrible guilt trip to place on a kid. Remember that in the end, the kid needs to leave you to move on in life to become a successful adult.

WHEN THE ADULT KID HAS BECOME A MOOCH:

So, what to do with the kids who are working little, going to school little, and not contributing? Change the rules. Tell them if they are not full time students, or working and going to school (making up full time),

they must pay rent! What a novel idea! I promise you
there is a magical place between $200 and $300 a
month where kids will say, "I am going to go live with
a friend." That's OK. They are supposed to leave. Let
them know they are still loved and reset the same
boundary. If they return because they have bombed
out with the new arrangement and cannot make it,
don't get sucked into taking care of them instead of
expecting them to take care of themselves. It is all
right to let them come home if you and your partner
agree, but do not give them a free ride. Expect them to
pay their way, just as before. Also, do not fall into the
trap of saying, "You can stay here until you get a job
and get on your feet." They will stay there and get on
your feet and will not be motivated to take responsibility for their lives. Instead, say, "You can stay here if
you get a job and share the expenses."

In addition, be sure kids pay their share of the
utilities and food. Toilet paper, soap, and soup all cost
you. Don't provide them necessities and amenities if
they are of adult age! They will not appreciate you for
it. In fact, they will have contempt for you until you
finally show them the door and they have to ultimately grow up.

When you try to set all these boundaries, they will
begin to snivel and pour on the guilt, or become
outraged at you. Worse yet, they will agree and then
not follow through with what you ask.

Get ready for some of the seductions for persuad-
ing you to continue to take care of them:

☺ You abused me as a child, and now that I am an
   adult, you are obligated to make it up to me.

☺ Your partner, partners spouse or spouses
   abused me, so you must make it up to me.

☺ I have special problems.

☺ My wife or husband, or the mother or father of my children has beat me up financially or physically and you have to make it up to me.

☺ If you do not take care of me, I will end up on the street or in jail, and it will be your fault (rather than my responsibility).

☺ I lost my job and have no money.

☺ I can't do life   it is too hard because of my special psychiatric problems.

Many kids should be offered crackers with their whine.

Now, in the middle of all this is the compassionate parent who is saying something like the following:

☺ The kid has had a rough life due to the divorce between his father and myself.

☺ The kid has incurred a lot of debt in college due to all the Master Cards sent to her by those darn Master Card companies, and I have to save her credit from ruin. (More about this in the next section.)

☺ The kid has a car payment, cannot make it and I have to save him from bad credit.

☺ The kid has gone through a terrible marriage (or relationship) and needs to come home to heal.

☺ The kid is coming off drugs, alcohol, cocaine, or all of the above (usually the case) and is trying to get on his feet, so we have to help him.

Helping the kid is the goal. So, help them to grow up.

Help them to be accountable for their debts, relationships, and past pain. When we do it for them, they do not do it for themselves.

SCENARIO #2: FACING THE DEBT OF ADULT KIDS

The willingness of auto companies, Master Card, Visa, and many other credit companies to allow young people to amass huge debts is a major trend in our current economy. I firmly believe these companies extend credit with an ulterior motive. A company which allows a young person to take on substantial debts knows full well that the parents will probably bail the kids out of their debt so that the kids will not end up with bad credit. If a kid's credit is slightly shaky, or she does not make enough money, the creditors come up with the infamous co-signer, which basically means your credit is affected if you do not make her payments for her. It is often the ploy of car dealers to come right to the end of a car purchases, and say, "I am sorry, you must to have a co-signer," even when you have driven the car off the lot and put miles on it for a few days!

One of our four kids was able to amass $30,000 worth of debt and walk away from every penny of it! Unfortunately (or perhaps fortunately), she now has disastrous credit. My wife and I fought with one another, and with her, for a number of years before we realized we had to let her experience the consequences of her mistakes. We did not create the debt, and we should not pay it back. The consequence of not paying money back is paying cash for future purchases. This is not the end of the kid's world.

Another came home to live following a painful relationship and went into the full-time party mode, with us paying the freight. When we demanded she pay rent, she moved out and is doing quite well today.

We are proud of her independence. Simple isn't it? I wish it were as easy to do as it is to describe. It Is painful!

The same principle holds true here as in all other situations in this book. Do not do for the kid what the kid can do for herself. If she ran up the debt, let her pay it. If she cannot pay it, the credit companies will not let her have more money. The accumulated debt will have to be paid back, no matter how slowly to save the borrower's credit.

If they go bankrupt, they may be asking to borrow your credit. This is A Very Bad Idea. If you pay the debt for them, they will run up another series of debts and you will be right back where you started, and they will not have learned the lesson about money. To borrow and use other people's money, you have to show financial integrity. If you don't, lenders will not loan to you.

A word about counseling here; Beware of people who counsel you or your kids about money who do not manage it well themselves. The management of money is a major issue in the maturity of each of us. Counselors, ministers, and therapists often have little or no training in this area. They specialize in a world of feelings, and financial issues are not related to feelings. Remember, to handle the money issues with your children you must Be Like The Bank, which does not care how you feel or whether you are the current or past president of the IGMATT-Club, ("I'll-Get-My-Act-Together-Tomorrow-Club").

Another related warning is to beware of half-way houses, hospitals, and other surrogate parenting facilities which are not working themselves out of a job. At some point in every adult child's life, the child needs to grow up and get a job. If you are paying a facility to take care of kid who is coming out of a drug or alcohol problem, there may not be an incentive for the facility to pass the responsibility for payment from you to the kid. Responsible facilities recognize this and place enormous pressure on the kid to get a job and become independent. If the kid fails to do so, they show them the door and encourage you as a parent to do the same thing.

It is possible for one family to have many children who are all in different stages of learning about money. One can have good credit, one bad, one getting worse, and one better. Whatever the case, you will produce Financial Invalids if you continue to bail them out. Let them fall on their own faces, and then let them pick themselves up.

One worthwhile intervention for an adult kid is sending the kid to the Consumer Credit Council, which is listed in the phone book of large cities. This agency, which operates for little or no charge to the user of the service, has been set up to help people who are too deep in debt. It provides an option to bankruptcy by restruc-turing the debt so the debtor can pay it back. It is not in the business to try to convince the parent to pay back the debts of the adult kids. In the mean time, no other credit is extended, allowing the debtor to gradually dig out and work on a new financial plan.

Many parents unwisely offer "loans" to their children to "help them." Often this does not help because the kid has avoided being "accountable" in the real financial world. The other major problem is that the kid will often not repay the debt, knowing full well the parent will do nothing about it, with the possible exception of making him feel guilty. This creates emotional distance and resentment among all members of the family. The other spouse who didn't approve of the deal is angry. The siblings are angry because they see the irresponsi-ble child receiving the money and not paying it back, and the borrower is angry at the parent for not letting him grow up. All of this is set in motion, as usual, in the name of love.

HERE ARE SOME ALTERNATIVE GUIDELINES ABOUT KIDS AND MONEY:

✔ When the kid does not make the car payment and you cosigned for it, take the car back. Why not? The bank would do this. Otherwise you are teaching the kid not to pay his debts.

✔ If a kid wants to borrow money to buy something or pay a debt, take something as real collateral: her stereo, her massive CD collection (which over the years has become larger than the inventory of some record stores), her gold earrings left her by Great-Aunt Harriet (better you than the pawn shop).

✔ If the kid does not pay rent, give him notice, then follow through by asking him to leave.

✔ Put the car in the kid's name on her 18th birthday. If she does not pay for the insurance on the car, don't pay it for her without some concrete arrangement. Let her pay it. If she doesn't, it's her problem.

✔ If a kid has to pay child support, let him. If he does not, he will visit the jail. Good therapy. It works every time, and it is a lot cheaper than conventional psychotherapy.

✔ If a kid gets a ticket, do not pay it. If she fails to pay it, she will learn what happens when she fails to do so. It doubles in price and goes into a warrant. Some day when she is least expecting it, she will be driving and be stopped by the police. When they discover the outstanding warrant, the kid will get a wake up call. It is all right to give her this information one time. After that, you are a nag   male or female (nagging has no gender boundaries).

DO NOT BAIL YOUR KIDS OUT OF JAIL!

They will not die in there. You and everyone else just think they will. We hear the horror stories all the time about jail. Heh, it is supposed to act as a deterrent. When most people experience it, they never want to return. That's the idea. Pay your tickets; don't drink and drive; don't fail to follow through with orders of the court, or you will find yourself in a temporary shelter you don't like.

SCENARIO # 3: WHEN YOUR PUPPIES: PARENTTING ABSENTEE PARENTING AND GRANDPARENTING

The passage from parenthood to grandparenthood is a significant one in all of our lives. Some people manage this better, some worse than others. While some families wait a long time to regenerate, others get right to it. At 12 or 13, children (who have passed into puberty) are capable of reproduction. Unfortunately, some of them fulfill this physiological capability long before they become adults.

Whatever your age, when your children reproduce, the important thing is whether or not you are Willing to be involved as grandparents and to what degree. Many grandparents today feel compelled rather than willing to involve themselves in child rearing for another generation. Grandparenting can be a very energy-intensive undertaking. Some undertake this job with joy and willingness. Some undertake it out of guilt and never question what they are doing to themselves or what message they are sending to the irresponsible parents.

There is a big difference between parenting and
grand- parenting. In grand parenting you have a
choice, and whatever you choose, no one has the right
to say you are wrong. You have every right to refuse
heavy involvement in the lives of your children's
children. Do not forget: To grandparent a child on a
full-time basis is a choice.

There is a law in the woods we must heed. Never
Mess With The Mother Bear. Some campers and
hikers have learned this the hard way. Mother bear
will make almost any personal sacrifice to save her
cubs. However, at some point in their growing up, she
runs them up a tree. She then disappears and they
never see her again.)

Many of us experience the instinctive feelings of the
mother bear. We will, at any sacrifice, protect our
young. In humans, this protective instinct is often as
strong in the father as in the mother. Some grandparents are no exception. Some of us as grandparents will
go to any length to protect our children's young. The
difference is that the legal right to function in the
parental role in humans rests primarily with the
biological mother and father, unless the courts have
removed this right. Even then, it is usually temporary
and conditional on things like their getting out of jail
or cleaning up from drugs and alcohol. Mothers then
have every right to take a child back whether the
grandparents want this or not. Ouch!

It is a sad thing to watch alternative parents take on
the job of raising a child , only to have the natural
parents take the child away at a later time. I spent the
first eight years of my life in a loving foster home.
When my twin sister and I were eight, my mother
returned and took us both. The pain of that separation
left an indelible scar on me that will be visible for the

rest of my life. It also left an indelible mark of love. Many persons beside myself have been nurtured by people other than their natural parents. This is one of the miracles of humankind and certain other mammals that we have the capacity to love other children, other animal species, and other fragile living things.

Just because parents are egg or sperm donors, does not mean they are willing or capable of raising us. Often many other people in the community must do so... aunts, uncles, friends, foster parents, stepparents, older brothers and sisters, neighbors, grandparents, and involved teachers.

The truth about many parents is that they are often not mature enough themselves to do the job. This is not always their fault. Sometimes parents are doing the best they can. They themselves have not had their own needs met, and frequently they lack the skill to do the job right. Sometimes it is all they can do to eke out a living. Sometimes the parents are growing up right along with the child. Later they may be more mature, sober, or willing to shoulder their parental responsibly. To continually blame one's parent for not performing his or her job perfectly is to let the parent live inside you rent-free.

Blame here serves no purpose and heavily burdens the blamer with resentment. We must forgive our caretakers not just for their sakes, but also for our own sakes. My forgiveness is an act of love done often by me and for me so I can be at peace with something I cannot change. Do not confuse forgiveness with accepting vulnerability. To forgive does not mean I can no longer set limits or establish boundaries for persons whom I consider toxic.

I must admit that when I had my first child I was 22 years old and terrified of the job. My mother was much younger when she took on the job, and now I can imagine how hard it must have been for her. I have met parents well into their thirties and forties, some of whom have already had other children, who are still terrified of this overwhelming job. They well should be, as it is the most difficult job we will ever do, and one of the most important.

There is a miracle taking place all over this country that therapists like myself have had the good fortune to see. It is the miracle of watching mothers and fathers, previously strung out on drugs and alcohol, get sober and reunite with their own children and parents. Our war on drugs will not be fought at our borders and won. It will be won by the thousands of us who have been to the dark side of life and then had our lives returned to us through sobriety.

Sober parents, with the right coaching from treatment programs, therapy, churches, and 12-step programs, are paving the way for a new generation of parents who are drug and alcohol free. Hokey or not, like Tiny Tim said, "God bless them one and all." The other aspect of this miracle lies in the fact that when the child of a recovering alcoholic or drug addict encounters a drug or alcohol problem, that child often gets sober sooner in his or her life than the parent. The parent has provided an image of the disease, as well as passed on a genetic predisposition in some cases, but has also provided an image of sobriety.

Some people cannot turn their backs on their grandchildren. If this is your situation, go for it. Just remember, you are heading for a difficult job. You are teaching your own child that he or she once again does not have to take responsibility for his or her actions. Remember, too, that part of your children's lives may well be the realization that they must get their acts together and responsibly parent the child they brought into the world. You are teaching your grandchildren that they have irresponsible parents to model themselves after. You may also be showing your spouse that you do not want to spend the next stage of your life with him or her alone.

This is not all negative. Some people love to grand-parent. I look forward to it. The irony of our lives as males is that by the time we are ready to become grandparents, we are often not as obsessed with our careers and other peripheral challenges. We are often more loving, attentive, and caring. This occasions dismay in our children, who often say, "Why couldn't you have been that way with me?" Maybe it's hormones. Whatever it is, there is often a qualitative difference between grandparents' nurturing and the way the grandparents acted with their own children. If you want to do the job, go for it, and don't let anyone hand you a guilt trip. Remember, you can be a Militant Parent and/or a Militant Grandparent. No matter, someone will probably take you on.

CHAPTER SEVEN

WHEN YOUR KID IS ON DRUGS

It really hurts when your kid is on drugs. I have "been there, done that, and have the T-Shirt." Double ouch! The only person who can understand this pain is the parent who has been through it. Even the kid does not feel the same pain, because he or she is high (or low) on the mind-altering substance.

Here are some facts and survival tips:

SURVIVAL TIP #1: ALCOHOL IS A DRUG.

When people talk about drug addiction, many fail to recognize this often-overlooked fact: Alcohol is the #1 drug problem in the nation. It is surprising that we don't all know this. There is more domestic violence, death behind the wheel, suicide, assault, and murder while under the influence of alcohol than associated with all the other drugs combined. Within every heroin user, cocaine user, and crack addict is a person using and abusing alcohol to some degree. Often, if addicts get off their drug of choice, they continue to drink, prolonging their drug addiction by migrating to a different drug. Also, alcohol acts as a bridge-drug for the return to a previously abused drug or illegal behavior.

If alcohol is a problem in your home, the first step you and your spouse can take is to stop using it. The "do as I say, not as I do" tack is a poor argument to a kid, who sees right through it. I promise you that you will have enough to focus on while dealing with your own drug use that you will not have to obsess about the kid so much.

You may be annoyed by this admonition, but experience has taught me that when teenagers and young adults are part of a treatment program which asks their parents to abstain from drugs and alcohol while the kid is in treatment, many positive changes take place within the family environment.

Asking a kid not to use any intoxicants such as alcohol or marijuana when we are abusing such substances ourselves does not a good role model make!

SURVIVAL TIP #2:   GET IN AND STAY IN A SUPPORT GROUP

There is safety in numbers, and there is also a lot of love and caring within support groups. People in support groups will show you the true meaning of community. No one is getting rich on them, at least not monetarily, but they offer a great wealth of experience, literature, and supporters who truly care. Try several groups until you find one you like. Consider affiliating with another church or synagogue in your community that has a ministry directed toward helping parents in need. If you cannot find one, start one. That is exactly how the founders of Togh Love, Alanon, Overcomers, and Families Anonymous started their mission to help other parents.

Stay close to the people who help you to work the program instead of telling you exactly what to do. It is you, and not they, who feel the consequences of your actions. Go with the people who lead you to the knowledge and wisdom of the group, and not the ones who have a cadre of "babies" who are all being told what to do and when to do it.

We foster a subtle change in our consciousness when we take responsibility for OUR decisions. We gain our own wisdom. Remember, the goal is to work ourselves out of a job with our kids. We must expect the same of our mentors. Find those who lead you to make your own constructive choices.

Finding a support group is as easy as picking up the phone book. There are listings for the following:

Tough Love (1-888-259-4140) A national group for parents having problems with kids.

Alanon (1-800-736-9805) See local phone directory for listing. Helpful when there is someone in your life whose drinking concerns you.

Families Anonymous (See local directory listing.) For family members who are concerned about a child's drinking or drug use.

Naronon (See local phone listings.) Helpful when a loved one or friend has a drug problem.

SURVIVAL TIP # 3: MOST DRUG USERS AND ALCOHOLICS USE A NUMBER OF DRUGS.

There is a term in drug parlance, "drug of choice." But in a pinch, most young drug users take whatever they can get. They also use nicotine, caffeine, and sugar like it's their last day on earth. Notice the similarity to us? Most Americans (4 out of 5) use caffeine. Many people still smoke. These are all mood-altering chemicals. If you don't think cigarettes are mood altering, just try being around someone who is trying to quit. I guarantee you, your mood will be altered just by being in proximity to such a person.

When drug addicts quit one drug, they usually migrate to another they are already using or they start a new one. This is why drug abuse is often referred to as A Desease Of Migration. With this in mind, you can either lecture kids on this fact, which is a bad tactic, or you can mind your own business and consider the following:

SURVIVAL TIP # 4: GOD DID NOT OFFER YOU AN INTERNSHIP!!!

Addicts and alcoholics do not like to be told what to do. This is an interesting life problem, because they desperately need to figure out what to do. Once you discover you can't tell them, unless they ask, the situation becomes a little clearer. This is not to say it gets easier. The game is for them to ask, and then to revolt against what you tell them. If this all seems a little crazy, welcome to the realities of chemical dependency and parenting. The fact is that the best help will probably not come from you. It will come from another addict or alcoholic who understands the game and does not let the addict get away with it.

I am a recovering alcoholic and drug addict. I cannot tell my kids what to do with drugs. I can only show them what worked for me. At the time of this writing, three of the four have found their way. The forth struggles daily, and I can only pray. My pain at seeing this adult child suffer is beyond the comprehension of most people, except another parent who has been through it. The powerlessness I feel in not being able to effect change in my own child hurts. But no matter how much you know about this disease, and no matter how long you have worked in the field as a therapist, teacher, lecturer, writer, or director of treatment programs, you are powerless to make people change. They must want to change. And they do... when they are ready. Of course it may not always be in the direction you would have chosen for them.

There is no book, person, support group, church, or lecture that can get you through this painlessly. We all must turn to our God and leave it in His hands. The destiny of our children is partly their choice... and partly His. Have faith. Many people have gone ahead of us. Many people will follow. People do recover. The only person who can make sure there is a recovery is you. The recovery which is accomplished is YOUR RECOVERY. It may or may not be the kid's.

SURVIVAL TIP #5: YOU CAN NOT MAKE KIDS DRINK OR USE. AND YOU CAN NOT STOP THEM FROM DRINKING OR USING

Don't believe it do you? None of us believes this in the beginning. The use of alcohol and other drugs by our children is cunning and baffling. We think we are the cause of their problem, and then we think we have to be the cause of the solution. We can be neither. We are powerless to change their behavior. I am not talking about a ten-year old here. At some point, however, in a kid's life, he or she takes over the control, and no matter what we do, we cannot stop them. We can, however, let them feel the full consequences of their behavior by neither blaming them, ourselves, our spouses, or anyone else. If the kid blames you or others, don't buy into it.

We can also refrain from enabling them:
- ✔ Don't bail them out of jail.
- ✔ Don't allow them to drive if they use drugs or alcohol.
- ✔ Don't bail them out financially when they lose their jobs and places to live due to their drug and alcohol abuse.

✔ Don't provide them with a "fall-guy" by
   lecturing them or blaming the other parent for
   their drug use.

✔ Do continue to tell them you love them (even if
   you don't like them.)

✔ Do go to a support group yourself.

✔ Do stay close to your spiritual base, if you have
   one, and have faith that a miracle can occur.

✔ Do seek a spiritual base if you don't have one.

✔ Do pray for them, yourself, and others who
   suffer.

SURVIVAL TIP # 6: LEARN ABOUT YOUR "CONTROL SLIPS"

A CONTROL SLIP is a term I use to help parents and
spouses understand the source of their frustration.
We cannot actually control or change another person.
Thinking we can is an illusion, a control slip. That
person must want to change. Occasionally, people in
recovery from any disease brought on by lifestyle
and poor choices (such as drug addiction and alco-
holism) will let us believe we are the ones responsible
for their change. This is an illusion. They must
accept responsibility for the change and the lack of
change. If not, they can blame us for their failures
and not take the credit for their successes.

A Person Experoencing A Conrtol Slip Is Saying, "I
Will Be All Right If Only You Will Follow My Plan
For YOur Life."

Possible control slips include:

✔ The kid is in the wrong career. Instead:
   They are in a career which is possibly a
   poor choice for them, but they will figure it
   out in their own time.

✔ The kid should quit smoking: Instead: She will quit smoking when she is ready, and it takes a number of tries for most people to make it.

✔ The kid should not marry this person. Instead: It is not my choice, but I am not the one doing the marrying. My job is to wish them happiness.

Think about this deeply, and it will save you and the people around you a great deal of heartache. We go in and out of control slips all day long with people—when we are on the road and other drivers are not doing it right; when we are at work and the other workers or bosses are not doing it right; in our interpersonal relationships, and, most importantly when, in our families, we meet disappointment rather than satisfaction because the persons in our families are not doing it right. Who made you the right and wrong monitor? How much heartache and unhappiness are you bringing yourself and the persons around you because you have a plan for their lives which they are not following. Learn to mind your own business. Granted, there are issues as parents we must monitor and control while children are young. But at some point, we must release them to make their own decisions, right or wrong. This does not mean we have no input. Wise council to another is an offering of options, not a command or obligation to do it the way we think it should be done.

Think of a faucet flowing as an analogy for parental control governing a seedling child. At some point in the child's life we must shut off the faucet and allow the child to assume responsibility for irrigating himself. If we don't, the child will resent our control, meddling, manipulation, and admonitions. To be truly wise with our children, we must learn to offer

suggestions and wisdom when it is asked for. Our
wise behavior must also include the willingness on
our part to allow the child to make the final decision.
Again, this is age specific.

When we are trying to control others, they sense it,
and it affects their dignity. Our children must have
the Dignity To Fail. That way they can learn from
their mistakes. When they have a revolt going against
us in an area of personal choice, the problem is
between ourselves and them, rather than between
themselves and themselves. This is non-productive.
Our important and most difficult battles in life are
with ourselves.

The strategy we develop to co-exist with their
decisions about their lives is critical to avoiding a
pattern of revolt. Sometimes, when we are unwisely
drawn into that pattern, we can get out by doing some
of the following:

✔ Keep telling them you love them, even if you
   are stepping over the bounds of their dignity.
   You may discover later that you have gone too
   far in control. It is always all right to
   apologize and remind them you love them.
   They will know you do, but it adds credence
   to your position when you can admit that you
   have gone too far.

✔ Learn to mind your own business about
   issues that are not yours to decide.

✔ Work on your change, tolerance, and
   acceptance of things you cannot change.
   Remember, there is enough to keep you busy
   for the rest of your life if you work on
   yourself. You are the example. Don't become
   obsessed with trying to change others. If you
   want to change someone, let it be you that you
   try to change. A habit. A compulsion. When
   taking on difficult challenges, let your

prayer be, *"God, change nothing in my life, change me."*

✔ Know that inevitably you will have to shut off the tap of parenting when your child is fast approaching adulthood. The sooner the better. This must be started during the child's younger life in little areas that eventually lead to larger issues. Work on issues such as self-reliance with money, following through with commitments, and accountability for bad driving habits.

✔ Know that your kids are also children of God. God will look out for them, and we are not HIM.

✔ Join a 12-step program, a church, or a support group. It is difficult to have CONTROL SLIPS when you are surrounded by people who are trying to overcome this in themselves also.

✔ Start a book study group with this book and other books which address parenting to assist the members in learning and establishing discussion.

CHAPTER EIGHT

HOPE FOR THE FUTURE

Families are amazingly resilient. The things a family can endure and overcome with love and faith are almost beyond human comprehension. When you are in the depths of victimization by an out-of-control kid, remember that that kid will probably some day grow up. If the kid refuses to make progress toward responsibility, you can step out of their lives until they change. A kid can also step out of your life. However, these periods of alienation usually don't last forever. We seek temporary separations because we need to survive our crises. Crises pass in a family like storms, droughts, and fame. Kids grow up. Parents change, and life goes on... in spite of our mistakes and confusion.

Have hope. Get help. Join a support group in your church or synagogue. Participate in a 12-step program. If you can't find a group, start one! The national groups will be glad to send you free literature. Pray for your kids if you can. Pray for yourself while you're at it.